Through
the
Forest

BY DAVID WAGONER

POETRY

Dry Sun, Dry Wind (1953)
A Place to Stand (1958)
The Nesting Ground (1963)
Staying Alive (1966)
New and Selected Poems (1969)
Riverbed (1972)
Sleeping in the Woods (1974)
Travelling Light (1976)
Collected Poems 1956–1976 (1976)
Who Shall Be the Sun? (1978)
In Broken Country (1979)
Landfall (1981)
First Light (1983)
Through the Forest: New and Selected Poems (1987)

NOVELS

The Man in the Middle (1954)
Money Money Money (1955)
Rock (1958)
The Escape Artist (1965)
Baby, Come on Inside (1968)
Where Is My Wandering Boy Tonight? (1970)
The Road to Many a Wonder (1974)
Tracker (1975)
Whole Hog (1976)
The Hanging Garden (1980)

EDITED

*Straw for the Fire: From the Notebooks
   of Theodore Roethke, 1943–1963* (1972)

Through
the
Forest

NEW AND
SELECTED POEMS,
1977–1987

by David
Wagoner

THE ATLANTIC
MONTHLY PRESS
New York

All the poems in this book were written between 1976 and 1986. The poems from *In Broken Country, Landfall,* and *First Light* appeared originally in the following journals: *Amicus Journal, American Poetry Review, Antaeus, Antioch Review, Atlantic Monthly, Bennington Review, Chicago Review, Concerning Poetry, Cutbank, Field, Georgia Review, Hampden-Sydney Poetry Review, Harper's, Harvard Review, Hudson Review, Indiana Review, Iowa Review, Kansas Quarterly, Kayak, Massachusetts Review, Memphis State Review, Mid-American Review, Missouri Review, Mss, The Nation, New England Review, The New Republic, The New Yorker, Ohio Review, Paris Review, Poetry, Poetry in the Cities, Poetry Miscellany, Prairie Schooner, Quest, Raccoon, Salmagundi, Telescope, Times Literary Supplement, Virginia Quarterly Review, Western Humanities Review.*

The poems appearing in book form for the first time were published originally in the following: "To the Last Man," *Antaeus;* "There," *Antioch Review;* "The Excursion of the Speech and Hearing Class," *Agni Review;* "Eulogy for Richard Hugo (1923–1982)," *Atlantic Monthly;* "Photographing a Rattlesnake," *Boston Review;* "Catching the Big One at Lone Lake," "Looking for Nellie Washington," *Kenyon Review;* "In Enemy Territory," "Securing a House," "At Peace," *The Literary Review;* "Coming Home Late with the Bad Young Man," "On Motel Walls," *The New Criterion;* "Five Dawn Skies in November," *The New Republic;* "Our Father," "The Model," "The Play," "Ode to Twelve Yards of Unscreened Fill Dirt," "Mockingbird," "For a Third Anniversary," "The Astronomer's Apprentice," *Poetry;* "The Track Scale Weigher," "My Father's Football Game," *Triquarterly;* "Sharp-shin," "In the Dream House," *Virginia Quarterly Review.*

FIRST EDITION

Library of Congress Cataloging-in-Publication Data

Wagoner, David
  Through the forest.

  I. Title.
PS3545.A345T5   1987   811'.54   87-927
ISBN 0-87113-154-4
ISBN 0-87113-153-6 (pbk.)

Published simultaneously in Canada
Printed in the United States of America

First Printing

Design by Laura Hough

*These poems are
for Robin
with all my love.*

❧ CONTENTS

ONE

One

❧ After the Speech to the Librarians

I was speaking to the Librarians,
And now I'm standing at the end of a road,
Having taken a wrong turn going home.
I don't remember what I said.
Something about reading and writing
And not enough about listening and singing.
The gate to this dude ranch is locked,
And a dozen riderless horses are browsing
On the hillside in the gold grass.
On a post, a marsh hawk is holding still,
One eye on me and one on the field
Where hundreds of sparrow-sized water pipits
Are darting and whistling to themselves.
Not even thinking of opening a thesaurus,
I say on behalf of the Librarians, *Beautiful.*

Beyond barbed wire, a cracked water tank
And a wrecked shed: you could wait there
A long time for a school bus.
Whoever locked the gate meant No Thank You,
Not Today, but it wasn't much use.
Everything is trespassing as easily
As the hazy sunlight and these burnt-gold-breasted birds
Taking their sweet time under the hawk's eye,
Even perching beside him, extremely happy
To be where they are and what they are,
And the horses with nothing on their backs
Have opened their own gates for the winter,
And the Librarians are going back to their books
In hundreds and hundreds of schools where children
Will be reading and writing and keeping quiet
Maybe and listening to how not to be so childish.

When I wasn't looking, the hawk flew suddenly,
Skimming the field, effortlessly graceful, tilting
And scanning at low level: he stops

Dead without slowing down, swivels
And drops into the grass, flashing white
And tawny, rises at full speed carrying nothing
And goes on soaring, slanting downhill
No higher than my head, making his sharp outcry.
The water pipits answer, thin as fence wire.
Isn't it wonderful not being dead yet?
Their breasts all hold the same air
As his and the softly whickering unsaddled horses'
And mine and the Librarians'
With which we all might sing for the children.

❦ *Sharp-shin*

He broke past the corners
Of our eyes before we could see, before
We could quite catch
Sight of him already beyond
The fence and the next yard and back
Again in full flight, the sharp-shinned
Hawk, an amber and slate streak
Through the morning air after
A blur of a pine siskin, zigzagging
But (like our eyes) not quite touching it, not quite
Taking it in a swirling S-curve
Through vine maple up in a flare
Of tail stripes and dark coverts
To a hemlock branch to perch
Dead still, his claws empty.

Still breathing, we waited. The towhees,
The song sparrows, the juncos
Huddled in thickets, and the quick yellow-
And-gray-streaked siskins flocked
Quivering in a fir tree,
Waiting. The whole broad yard
Fell silent, and nothing moved
Anywhere, not even the one cloud.

He waited too, his breast the shade
Of dead leaves, his blue-gray wings
Folded like bark. The dimmed fire coals
Of his eyes held all of us
There, slow minute
After minute, where we were.

Finally, gradually, one siskin forgot
Where it was, where it had been and why
It had ever been afraid, remembered
Simply wanting to be

Somewhere else that moment and flew
At last from there only
To there in the open, and instantly
So swiftly nothing could know
Exactly when he began the sharp-shin
Burst out of cover around
And up in a tight swerve, struck
Without a pause, and was gone
Deep through the green tree-crown
That made no stir or murmur,
And all fell still once more
While out of his sharp talons
The sharper hook of his beak
Took its share of spring.

❦ *Return to the Swamp*

To begin again, I come back to the swamp,
To its rich decay, its calm disorder,
To alders with their reddening catkins, to hummocks
Of marsh grass floating on their own living and dead
Abundance, and wait on the shore. From my shallow angle,
Even shallows turn solid: a cast-off sky,
A rough sketching of clouds, a bearable version
Of the sun in a mist, the upside-down redoubling
Of cattails, and my eyes, shiftless,
Depending on surface tension like water striders.

What did I hope to find? This crystal-gazing
Brings me no nearer what the mergansers know
Or the canvasbacks keeping their distance or the snipes
Whirring away from me, cackling, their beaks down-turned,
Heads cocked for my false alarm as they swivel
Loudly and jaggedly into the next bog.
Here among shotgun shells and trampled blackberries,
How can I shape, again, something from nothing?

Edgy and mute, I wait at the edge,
And a bass taking a fly—a splashing master,
Ringmaster of refracted light—remakes the world,
Rippling out beautiful exchanges of stress
And yield, upheaval and rearrangement, scattering
And then regathering the shards of the day,
And suddenly near, there, near in the water
Where he's been floating motionless all this hour,
The hump-browed bullfrog staring at me close-mouthed,
Fixing on me his green, princely attention.

The Author of American Ornithology *Sketches a Bird, Now Extinct*

(Alexander Wilson, Wilmington, N.C., 1809)

When he walked through town, the wing-shot bird he'd hidden
Inside his coat began to cry like a baby,
High and plaintive and loud as the calls he'd heard
While hunting it in the woods, and goodwives stared
And scurried indoors to guard their own from harm.

And the innkeeper and the goodmen in the tavern
Asked him whether his child was sick, then laughed,
Slapped knees, and laughed as he unswaddled his prize,
His pride and burden: an ivory-billed woodpecker
As big as a crow, still wailing and squealing.

Upstairs, when he let it go in his workroom,
It fell silent at last. He told at dinner
How devoted masters of birds drawn from the life
Must gather their flocks around them with a rifle
And make them live forever inside books.

Later, he found his bedspread covered with plaster
And the bird clinging beside a hole in the wall
Clear through to already-splintered weatherboards
And the sky beyond. While he tied one of its legs
To a table leg, it started wailing again

And went on wailing as if toward cypress groves
While the artist drew and tinted on fine vellum
Its red cockade, gray claws, and sepia eyes
From which a white wedge flowed to the lame wing
Like light flying and ended there in blackness.

He drew and studied for days, eating and dreaming
Fitfully through the dancing and loud drumming
Of an ivory bill that refused pecans and beetles,

Chestnuts and sweet-sour fruit of magnolias,
Riddling his table, slashing his fingers, wailing.

He watched it die, he said, with great regret.

❧ *A Remarkable Exhibition*

*Its diving ability in dodging at the flash of a gun is well
known. I once saw a remarkable exhibition of this power
by a loon which was surrounded by gunners in a
small cove on the Taunton River.*
—Arthur Cleveland Bent, *Life Histories of North
American Diving Birds,* 1919

It was remarkable, that day on the river
When eight gentlemen fowlers in tweeds and gaiters,
Some firmly on shore and some wading through rushes,
Put a loon to the test.
A light mist hovered in shreds, but for all intents
It was a commonplace morning, sunlit and windless,
Affording a clear view of the clear water
And its reflective surface.
Their guns were all breech-loaded, their aim steady,
And though they varied as gunners from indifferent
To expert, when the loon appeared out of nowhere
Beside them suddenly
At such close range, it seemed impossible
A bird of its size could dodge so many volleys
From unforeseeable angles more than a moment.
Across that cove
The sound of their guns went crackling and echoing
Under the pines, reechoing and colliding
Like the eccentric ripples that broke reflections
Around the loon's white breast
And starry back. It lifted its dark neck
And darker head and beak to go arching under,
And every time it plunged, they thought it was dying,
But it would rise
Again whole minutes later unnaturally
Far off, unexpectedly, in unpredictable
Directions, breathe, swivel and arch to dive
Again, and be gone.
They were genuinely amazed at a performance

That round for round matched theirs. It lasted longer
Than any of them could agree on through that winter
Over their hearthstones
When they recounted the tale and their cartridges
And tried to guess the mechanics of its defense
Aside from stubbornness and web-footed power
And those amber eyes
They couldn't help recollecting: how could they be
Magic enough to avoid eight shotguns flashing
As long as all that and still, as they finally were,
Be closed in death?

℣ *Thoreau and the Snapping Turtle*

[It] looked not merely repulsive, but to
some extent terrible even as a crocodile . . .
a very ugly and spiteful face.
—Thoreau, *Journal*, May 17, 1854.

As his boat glided across a flooded meadow,
He saw beneath him under lily pads,
Brown as dead leaves in mud, a yard-long
Snapping turtle staring up through the water
At him, its shell as jagged as old bark.

He plunged his arm in after it to the shoulder,
Stretching and missing, but groping till he caught it
By the last ridge of its tail. Then he held on,
Hauled it over the gunwale, and flopped it writhing
Into the boat. It began gasping for air

Through a huge gray mouth, then suddenly
Heaved its hunchback upward, slammed the thwart
As quick as a spring trap and, thrusting its neck
Forward a foot at a lunge, snapped its beaked jaws
So violently, he only petted it once,

Then flinched away. And all the way to the landing
It hissed and struck, thumping the seat
Under him hard and loud as a stake-driver.
It was so heavy, he had to drag it home,
All thirty pounds of it, wrong side up by the tail.

His neighbors agreed it walked like an elephant,
Tilting this way and that, its head held high,
A scarf of ragged skin at its throat. It would sag
Slowly to rest then, out of its element,
Unable to bear its weight in this new world.

Each time he turned it over, it tried to recover
By catching at the floor with its claws, by straining
The arch of its neck, by springing convulsively,
Tail coiling snakelike. But finally it slumped
On its spiky back like an exhausted dragon.

He said he'd seen a cut-off snapper's head
That would still bite at anything held near it
As if the whole of its life were mechanical,
That a heart cut out of one had gone on beating
By itself like clockwork till the following morning.

And the next week he wrote: *It is worth the while
To ask ourselves . . . Is our life innocent
Enough? Do we live* inhumanely, *toward man
Or beast, in thought or act? To be successful
And serene we must be at one with the universe.*

*The least conscious and needless injury
Inflicted on any creature is
To its extent a suicide. What peace—
Or life—can a murderer have? . . . White maple keys
Have begun to fall and float downstream like wings.*

*There are myriads of shad-flies fluttering
Over the dark still water under the hill.*

❧ *To a Farmer Who Hung Five Hawks on His Barbed Wire*

They saw you behind your muzzle much more clearly
Than you saw them as you fired at the sky.
You meant almost nothing. Their eyes were turning
To more important creatures hiding
In the grass or pecking and strutting in the open.
The hawks didn't share your nearsighted anger
But soared for the sake of their more ancient hunger
And died for it, to become the emblem
Of your estate, your bloody coat-of-arms.

If fox and raccoon keep out, your chickens may spend
Fat lives at peace before they lose
Their appetites, later on, to satisfy yours.
You've had strange appetites now and then,
Haven't you. Funny quickenings of the heart,
Impulses not quite mentionable
To the wife or yourslf. Even some odd dreams.
Remember that scary one about flying?
You woke and thanked the dawn you were heavy again.

Tonight, I aim this dream straight at your skull
While you nestle it against soft feathers:
You hover over the earth, its judge and master,
Alert, alive, alone in the wind
With your terrible mercy. Your breastbone shatters
Suddenly, and you fall, flapping,
Your claws clutching at nothing crookedly
End over end, and thump to the ground.
You lie there, waiting, dying little by little.

You rise and go on dying a little longer,
No longer your heavy self in the morning
But light, still lighter long into the evening
And long into the night and falling
Again little by little across the weather,

Ruffled by sunlight, frozen and thawed
And rained away, falling against the grass
Little by little, lightly and softly,
More quietly than the breath of a deer mouse.

✢ The Horsemen

All day we followed the tracks of the wild horses
On foot, taking turns at resting,
Eating our cold food as we walked each way
They turned to escape us. They disappeared
Sometimes behind rough-shouldered ridges, up canyons,
But we hurried after them and found them
Too soon for grazing. They swam rivers
That might have made them safe from wolves
But not from *our* hunger: it was behind our eyes
And not in our mouths. As we came nearer, nearer,
Their heads would turn to us, then turn
Away, they would go away aimlessly,
Hating our smell as we loved theirs and hating
The sight of us as we loved theirs, the headstrong
Round-rumped tangle-maned light-footed
Windy-tailed horses who would belong to us.

Already, others of our slow kind were flying
Above four hooves, their feet leaving the earth
Like birds flying as far as we could go
In five of our old sleeps. Now following after
At evening, we gave them no rest, gave nothing
But hunger and that other emptiness:
Fear of our strangeness. Some of us slept by water
While they stood in the distance, darkening,
Smelling it with dry nostrils, waiting to drink
As deep as the coming night but seeing us waiting
There for something they must have known was their hearts
And their whole lives to come.

In the morning, they were kneeling, lying down, rising
And trotting again, then slowing, walking no faster
Than we kept walking after them. They stumbled
And fell once more and stayed where they were

As if dying, their white-flecked mouths
And white-cornered eyes all turning
As we touched them on their trembling withers to tell them
What they were, what they would learn from us.

❧ *Posing with a Trophy*

Lying on the ground, your bear
Or cougar will look small, no matter
Where you stand in the picture,
Even putting your foot
In a time-honored position
On its carcass. Your trophy
Will loom much larger
If hoisted into the air
By its hind legs (never
The front legs or the neck: it will loll
Backwards or seem to strangle).

What your future admirers
(You hope) will wish to see
Is what you had to do
With a dangerous predator.
Your place is the background
Where, by comparison, you'll appear
Smaller and more suitable
For framing, holding your rifle
At a casual angle, perhaps kneeling
To suggest reverent fatigue,
But above all never trying
To look more masterful
Than you are, simply aiming
A smile into the distance
Where good things come to an end.

A shot in living color
Under glass on the wall
Will reveal, like taxidermy,
Whatever was on your mind
Or in your mouth (the teeth
Of the evidence) speechlessly
Like the snarl beside you.

✌ *Being Herded Past the Prison's Honor Farm*

The closer I come to their huge black-and-white sides, the less
Room there is in the world for anything but Holsteins.
I thought I could squeeze past them, but I'm stuck now
Among them, dwarfed in my car, while they plod gigantically
To pasture ahead of me, beside me, behind me, cow eyes
As big as eightballs staring down at another prisoner.

They seem enormously pregnant, bulging with mash and alfalfa,
But their low-slung sacks and rawboned high-rise rumps
   look insur-
Mountable for any bull. One sideswipes my fender
And gives it a cud-slow look. What fingers would dare
Milk those veiny bags? Not mine. I'm cowed. My hands
On the steering wheel are squeezing much too tight to be
   trusted.

They all wear numbers clipped to their ears. They're going to
   feed
Behind barbed wire like a work gang or, later, like solitaries
Stalled in concrete, for the milk of inhuman kindness.
They clomp muddily forward. Now splatting his boots down
Like cowflops, the tall black numbered trusty cowpoke tells me
Exactly where I can go, steering me, cutting me out of the herd.

❧ Bears

Out of shadows as deep as shadows
In the woods, the bears come swaying
On their hind legs, the black pads
Of forepaws reaching forward, their foreheads
Higher than all the men now running
Behind them into the charmed circle,
Into the ring and the glaring spotlight,
Now pausing, lifting their muzzles, turning
To a blare of horns, they begin dancing
At the ends of leashes, their fur gleaming
All shades of fallen leaves by moonlight,
Up on red globes and walking, not falling
Off, they waddle steadily, swiftly
To the feet of silver trees and climb them
To other trees, descending, they swivel
Firesticks in their claws, they ride
On wheels so surely, so heavily
They seem to spiral downward without
Stopping, and now they are swaying away
On sawdust to drumbeats, to applause
Like heartbeats while men are running behind them
Becoming shadows again among shadows.

❧ Games

The children from the nursery school are running
Slowly, zigzaggedly on the grass at the zoo,
Trying to catch the chickens that run free
Among the bushes and always get away.

The game is called Chasing Something. You play it
Squawking and clucking, wonderfully unhappy
Not to be able to touch those feathers ruffling
And flapping, squawking back at you out of fear.

You wear your name and the name of your keeper
And don't pay any attention to each other
Or to lions or llamas or boas or kangaroos.
You want your game to be right out in the open

Where you can reach for it with friendly fingers
And crow out loud to say how eager you are,
How hungry to learn a game called Catching Something.
But if you catch it, then what do you do?

Do you start a zoo and fill it with wild playthings
Waiting behind bars to look at children
Chasing more chickens under the maple trees?
You don't catch anything yet. Keepers catch *you.*

They make you sit together and play Yelling
And Eating and Drinking and Dropping Sandwiches.
The chickens gather around you quietly
And play their game called Come to the Picnic.

❧ *Washing a Young Rhinoceros*

Inside its horse-high, bull-strong, hog-tight fence
It will stand beside you in a concrete garden,
Leaning your way
All thousand pounds of its half-grown body
To meet the water pouring out of your hose
The temperature of September.

And as slowly its patina (a gray compounded
Of peanut shells and marshmallows, straw and mud)
Begins to vanish
From the solid rib cage and the underbelly
Under your scrub brush, you see, wrinkled and creased
As if in thought, its skin

From long upper lip to fly-whisk gleam in the sun,
Erect ears turning backwards to learn how
You hum your pleasure,
And eyelashes above the jawbone hinges
Fluttering wetly as it waits transfixed
(The folds at the four leg-pits

Glistening pink now) for you never to finish
What feels more wonderful than opening
And closing its empty mouth
Around lettuce and grapes and fresh bouquets of carrots
And cabbage leaves, what feels as good to desire
As its fabulous horn.

❧ Seeds

By night they climbed the dead sunflower stalks in my workroom
Like a circus act: the field mice, making their own percussion
Among dry leaves, spotlit by car-light and starlight,
Juggling the seeds still left in those corollas, balancing
High against books, nibbling and hoarding, spilling their shells
Over stained manuscripts, their perches bowing, wavering
Further, still further. But I was no claque for an encore.

So the sunflowers had to go. They suffered the last dust
To be knocked out of their roots, then trailed me to their
    birthplace,
A sundeck, where I shucked their seeds into a sack.
Their stalks and crook-necks had toughened through years of
    performing
As emblems of constant, hardheaded, sun-filled brooding
For this paper-scratcher who stared at them each morning,
    hoping
To learn their ways. I buried them over the side in a sea of ivy.

Now a pair of chickadees is at work on those same seeds.
They eat their fill and hide the rest in wild places
Where they'll sprout in the next rain: the cracks of furniture,
Under saucers, in bamboo blinds, behind peeling birchbark,
In the vacant eyes of a horse skull, in a whale's backbone.
Black-and-white birds, the color of sunflower seeds and field
    mice,
Even ink and paper, are cramming darkness with light.

✿ *Nuthatch*

Quick, at the feeder, pausing
Upside down, in its beak
A sunflower seed held tight
To glance by chestnut, dust-blue,
White, an eye-streak
Gone in a blurred ripple
Straight to the cedar branch
To the trunk to a crevice
In bark and putting it
In there, quick, with the others,
Then arrowing straight back
For just one more all morning.

❧ *Peacock Display*

He approaches her, trailing his whole fortune,
Perfectly cocksure, and suddenly spreads
The huge fan of his tail for her amazement.

Each turquoise and purple, black-horned, walleyed quill
Comes quivering forward, an amphitheatric shell
For his most fortunate audience: her alone.

He plumes himself. He shakes his brassily gold
Wings and rump in a dance, lifting his claws
Stiff-legged under the great bulge of his breast.

And she strolls calmly away, pecking and pausing,
Not watching him, astonished to discover
All these seeds spread just for her in the dirt.

❧ *Mockingbird*

A campus prophet with his mouth to a bullhorn,
Shouting and shorting out, gives me the message:
God wants to hear from me. God is demanding
Attention, attention, and my soul to go
With it, no matter how hard I try to hide it.

But suddenly one of His more gifted creatures
In my other ear becomes His competition
This morning, being far more persuasive:
On a stump, its ecumenical voice upraised
To cut across the concessions and flight plans
Of all schismatics, a mockingbird
Starts singing the up-slurred *wheat wheat wheat*
What cheer of a cardinal more spiritedly
Than any cardinal, a jumble of trills
From the airs of myrtle warblers, a quarrel of jays,
The double-bowing of meadowlarks, piercing *may-rees*
Check check and double *check* of boat-tailed grackles,
A rehearsal of the Ninety-nine Mysteries
Of the Kingdom of Incarnation, and with each passage,
Each shift of character, its gray throat pulses,
Its breast surges, and its clear visions
Of Otherness come spilling over the thresholds
Of tongue and beak, while with its wings half spread
For shelter or flight, it reenacts the legends
And transformations of all its lesser kindred.

And getting into this act of faith, I whistle
Five tuneless notes lamely at random,
A Listen-to-*Me,* an amateur call for help,
And without a pause, in the midst of all it knows
By heart already, it gives me back my song
In the sincerest form of mockery: as revised,
Perfected, and immortalized by a master.

❧ *Meditation on the Union Bay Garbage Fill*

There would be classrooms here by now if the inspired garbage
(Fifty years of waste dumped by our City Fathers)
Hadn't stayed alive, sending its swamp gas
Through cracks and hummocks to flicker blue in the night,
    turning
Golf tees on the driving range into bunsen burners.

Already it's *my* classroom: I lunch here with marsh hawks
And chipping sparrows, quails and cinnamon teals, and listen
For something beyond the burr of traffic, having done my share
Of adding to this rubble over my years and years,
Of laying this foundation for wildlife.

The sign says it's a sanctuary. Dogs must be kept on leashes.
On mine, I stare at the tentative grass, a place for hard times
Where whatever wants to grow will have to make it
In the worst way, wrestling for root-room in gravel and broken
    glass
Or clawing and singing dead to rights for a nesting ground.

I wait my turn, a man grown desperate to be grown,
To be filled, to be fulfilled before it's too late
Even to hope for a sign from barn swallows, these masters
Of aimless, unpremeditated, single-minded grace, now flying
Carelessly through barbed wire, diving and doubling

Back at their own moment's notice over the yellow broom
And skimming across the crows' hodge-podgy gambits,
Their forked tails more delicate and precise than the glance of
    an eye
That can only follow the blue sheen of their curvetting
After the fact, hopelessly laggard but still dreaming

Here in the half-dead of summer
Of taking their ways above this flammable earth.

✤ Sitting by a Swamp

Minutes ago, it was dead:
This swamp when I first came
Fell still as if poisoned,
The air expiring, cattails
Bent and brought to nothing
By the motionless water.

Now first the sunfish rising
To touch the underface
Of the pool, a muttered frog-call,
And out of the willow roots
From crushed stems and stubble
The *chap* of a marsh wren,

From a thicket a fox sparrow
Taking me in, one eye
At a wary time, where I wait
To be what they want me to be:
Less human. A dragonfly
Burns green at my elbow.

❧ Bittern

Neck drawn in, dark shoulders
Hunched, the bittern alone
Among marsh reeds, its beak
A splinter pointed at clouds,
The stump of its brown body
Motionless, till now one gust
Of wind moves the dead stalks
Around it, the bittern swaying
Slowly like reeds, the long thin
Streaks of its breast moving
In time with wind, then slowing
To stillness, standing (barely
There) by water, waiting.

❧ The Death of a Cranefly

It falls from the air
Stricken, spiraling
Lamely, already dying,
Its arched inch and a half
Of body trailing
The long disjointed-seeming
Legs out of sunlight
Onto the pond's dark water
Where swiftly a water strider
Clings to it, rippling
And skimming away with it over
Reflections of yellow leaves,
Holding one amber
Lace-ribbed lifeless wing
Aloft (a small sail
Disappearing among the quiet
Inlets of milfoil)
As buoyantly as a lover.

✣ *Winter Wren*

It knows each leaf, it darts
Under each leaf so swiftly
It seems here there
Not there now clinging one
Instant to a frond, its quick
Brief thumb of a body gone
With a tail-flick among moss
And under the green roots
Of a stump in rain as soft
As moss and back again
Where suddenly it holds still
At the loud warning call
Of a thrush, long minute
After minute, motionless,
Becoming no wren now
But streaks of buff and umber
Beyond it, the stiff stems
And star-claws of dead leaves,
Disappearing no matter how
Hard my eyes may stare
At where it quickened,
Then faded to nothing
On earth as plain as daylight.

❧ Marsh Hawk

Along the split-rail fence, no higher
    Than a man standing, the hawk comes
Flying as jaggedly as the rails,
    Its wings touching them nearly the color
Of trees turned into weather
    By years, dead silent now, one wingbeat
For every swerve, eyes scanning
    The grass for gray deer mice
Under the leaning posts, catching
    No shadow in that light as gray
As the sea wind, hearing nothing
    As sharply soft as its sudden cry, flying
Away, fence-riding crookedly, tilting
    From field to marsh to darkness.

❧ *Kingfisher*

The blunt big slate-blue dashing cockaded head
Cocked and the tapering thick of the bill
Sidelong for a black eye staring down
From the elm branch over the pool now poised
Exactly for this immediate moment diving
In a single wingflap wingfold plunging
Slapwash not quite all the way under
The swirling water and upward instantly
In a swerving spiral back to the good branch
With a fingerling catfish before the ripples
Have reached me sitting nearby to follow it
With a flip of a shake from crestfeathers to white
Bibchoker down the crawhatch suddenly
Seeing me and swooping away cackling
From the belt streaked rusty over the full belly.

❧ Golden Retriever

Dew-soaked and bleary-eyed with the smells of the field,
He zigzags out of cheatgrass and wild roses
And fallen thistles, as gold, as ragged, his tongue
Lolling, nose high, his breath trailing a mist
Over the empty weed-crowns as he drinks in
The whole morning at once, around his neck
A broken chain that follows him over hummocks
By sunlight on the sheen of cobwebs binding
The dead spikelets of grass and their living stems
And down through sedge and rushes along the creek
And up among brambles and arches of blackberry
To disappear in the light-filled field again.

☙ *Loons Mating*

Their necks and their dark heads lifted into a dawn
Blurred smooth by mist, the loons
Beside each other are swimming slowly
In charmed circles, their bodies stretched under water
Through ripples quivering and sweeping apart
The gray sky now held close by the lake's mercurial threshold
Whose face and underface they share
In wheeling and diving tandem, rising together
To swell their breasts like swans, to go breasting forward
With beaks turned down and in, near shore,
Out of sight behind a windbreak of birch and alder,
And now the haunted uprisen wailing call,
And again, and now the beautiful sane laughter.

❧ *Wading in a Marsh*

Nothing here in this rain-fed marsh
Has known the sun on the far side of the mountain
Except by the hearsay of the moon
Or the glinting of clouds and snow through cedar boughs,
And by this hand-me-down light I wade,
Uncertain of every surface preoccupied
By milfoil and watercress, the floating
Intricate uncannily green beds
Of water starwort whose leaves allow
No reflection of mine, not even their own.

My rake-handle staff goes first, searching
For footholds in the moss under the water,
In the soft debris of needles and spikerush
And mud and the good lost lives of bur reeds,
And my feet follow, slow as the spawn of tree frogs.
The water-logged hemlock logs give way
Underfoot as easily as the earth they've turned to,
And my staff, at times, reaches down to nothing
As deep as I am tall. I don't go there.

Even with something seemingly lasting
Under me, I sink if I stand still,
Learning the underlying answer
Of swamps as unforgettably as my name:
To stand is to sink, to move is to rise
Again, and nothing at all has died in the winter
Without being reborn. The duckweed
Drifting against my thighs is rootless, unnerved,
Immortal, a cold companion
To be cupped in the palm and then let go
Here in Barr Mountain's permanent shadow.

I see what to say: this marsh that holds me
Is the climax of a lake, shallowing, dying,
Filled with the best endeavors of pondweeds,

The exploring and colonizing shapes of a world
Too good at living for its own good,
But in this man-made silence, while wrens and kinglets
Decide what I am and slowly excuse me
For being a moving object with much less use
Than a stump, I learn why I came here
Out of order: in order to find out how to belong
Somewhere, to change where all changing
Is a healing exchange of sense for sense.

I start to sink, I take a step,
The mud puts up with me momentarily,
And three wrens at once from three directions
Burst into songs as wildly interwoven
As white water crowfoot tripling itself in shade.
I have to stand still to listen. By the time
I've heard the spruce grouse drumming and drumming
Under the wrensongs, vibrant as memory,
I begin to sink. One winter wren
Appears from a literal nowhere: in her beak
A stark-green writhing caterpillar
Airborne ahead of its time. In an instant, she scans
The parts of me still above water,
Then vanishes among a tangle of roots
To feed her young. Far overhead
Sunlight crosses the treetops like crownfire,
And the last snow of a new spring
Melts as it falls, turning to other stars.

❧ *Whisper Song*

Listening and listening
Closely, you may hear
(After its other
Incredibly clear song)
The one the winter wren
Sings in the thinnest of whispers
More quietly than soft rain
Proclaiming almost nothing
To itself and to you,
And you must be
Only a step away
To hear it even faintly
(No one knows why
It will sing so softly),
Its tiny claws
Braced for arpeggios,
Its dark eyes
Gleaming with a small
Astonishing promise,
Its beak held open
For its hushed throat,
Whispering to itself
From its mysterious heart.

❧ *Chorus*

That rain-strewn night in the woods, the *chorus, chorus*
Of the green tree frogs called us
And led us by flashlight far from our firelight
Over and down a logging road to the marsh,

And they kept singing as green as the half-frozen
Hemlock branches we brushed slowly among,
As high and thin as the air we tried to hold
As breath among mountains, as thin

And clear as the ice our boots were breaking
Gently, each step a pale-green croaking
Of its own, as we came nearer and nearer where
They had risen out of cold graves to the cold

At the brittle edge of winter broken toward spring
To make their music over a cold spawning,
To choir all night after night, telling each other
We lived at the end of summer, we live

Here again and again. As we came closer,
The singing ended, suddenly went silent
At a single pulsing throatbeat. Nothing but wind
And sleet made any sound over the marsh.

We turned our light away. We waited longer
And longer in darkness, shivering like the reeds
Beyond us, chilled as the film of ice at our feet,
Forgetting all words, and the first voice began

Again, far off, and slowly the green others
Nearby began their hesitant answers, their answers
Louder and clearer chorused around us
As if we belonged there, as if we belonged to them.

❧ *Five Dawn Skies in November*

1

At the roots of clouds a cutworm hollowing
The night, its eyes moonblind.

2

On the sheen of a lake the moment before wind,
Before rain, a loon floating asleep.

3

As smoothly blurred as (seen through water) a marten
Rippling among marshgrass.

4

Deepening into winter, a bear at her burrow
At first light on the first light snow.

5

A salmon stranded on stones, its mouth still opening
And closing toward the river.

❧ Return to the River

Through streaming sunlight and rain, surging, the humpback
　salmon
Climb home again, fins cutting the swift water
From shallows to pools
And up long drifts to rapids, their beaklike jaws once more
Tasting the truth of their first and final spawning—
Among them, these three holding
Where a female on her side is flailing her body ragged
On the nesting stones, her sleek jade tail gone white
As the foam around her,
And the four all suddenly yielding, surrendering to the current,
Swerving and yawing faster than it downstream,
Rehearsing their deaths,
But as suddenly turning, returning, hovering (like gulls
Playing the wind's hard game), one scarred near the eye,
The round clear staring eye,
By a fisherman's gaff or a seal or the teeth of a killer whale
In the moons of his salt life, the female thrashing
Again and again at the nest,
And the falling alder leaves skimming among them, the sky
Falling in gray-blue pieces fluttering shoreward
Like a hatch of mayflies,
And the males all holding, swaying above and behind her,
　waiting
For days for their instant, while the sun sinks deep and rises,
Scattering salmon-light.

❧ *Watching the Harbor Seals*

They float erect, their heads out of the water,
And then slip under
Gently without a ripple, feeding together
And moving near the shore
Of Dungeness Bay at the bright end of summer,
The blue-green shimmer
Of sea-bedded sky and sky-bedded sea the color
Of both, of neither,
Of what lies lost in our eyes like the birth of weather,
And the gulls hover
Above this drifting feast of eleven harbor
Seals, long-calling over
The cormorants diving among them, every fish-catcher
Silent, each scavenger
Screaming and turning, the glistening fur
And each glistening feather
In its place under the sun. The seals' eyes stare
Toward us without fear,
Mildly and calmly, knowing what we are:
The ones who suffer
There on the dry stones in the empty air
From a different hunger,
Who stand and wait, who simply watch and wonder,
Holding each other.

Sequence:
The Journey

※

※ Finding the Right Direction

Those times when too much stands between you and the sky—
Tree crowns and clouds or mist—when the hidden sun
Makes nothing of your shadow
To guide you south, you turn to stones, to slopes and trees,
To flowers, even to birds for your directions:
Cutting across bedrock,
The scars of glacial drift all point the same hard way
To mark the graveyard of ice which trundled boulders
Grindingly up hills
And, gouging abrupt drop-offs, tumbled them over and over
And left them strewn like markers, blunt in smooth fields,
While it melted south
On one straight, glittering journey which you may follow now
Rejoicing toward the end of your own ice age,
Sunbound and shrinking,
Or if the brush grows dense and your unmindful eyes
Can't choose between the dextrous and sinister,
See, the lightest branches,
The thickest, hardest bark most deeply grooved, the heaviest
Roots of old trees will stand to the bitter north,
Braced against winter,
And even the newly dead will show where not to go:

The center of decay lies out of sunlight.
Young trees lean *with* you
Like the new grass in this clearing where you've stumbled,
    seeing
Wildflowers sharing your clouds, but staring southward
For the certain return
Of what once brought them to light and, look, this empty cabin
At the edge of it, unhinged by years of weather,
Has under the southern eaves
Your surest compass, expecting a break in the gray of morning:
A swallow's nest clinging to next to nothing
Like you, beginning now.

❧ *Walking in Broken Country*

Long after the blossoming of mile-wide, fire-breathing roses
In this garden of dead gods when Apache tears
Burst out of lava
And after the crosshatched lightning and streambeds cracking
Their sideslips through mid-rock, after burnishing wind,
Your feet are small surprises:
Lurching down clumps of cinders, unpredictably slipshod,
And gaining your footholds by the sheerest guesswork,
You make yourself at home
By crouching, by holding still and squinting to puzzle out
How to weave through all this rubble to where you're going
Without a disaster:
One dislocation, one green-stick fracture, and all your bones
May fall apart out of sympathy forever.
In this broken country
The shortest distance between two points doesn't exist.
Here, straight lines are an abstraction, an ideal
Not even to be hoped for
(As a crow flies, sometimes) except on the briefest of terms:

Half a step on legs, after which you slump,
Swivel, or stagger.
You cling to surfaces feebly in a maze without a ceiling,
A whole clutch of directions to choose among
From giddy to earthbound,
Where backtracking from dead ends is an end in itself.
Through this clear air, your eyes put two and two
Together, take them apart,
And put them together again and again in baffling pieces,
Seeing the matter of all your sensible facts
Jumbled to the horizon.

❧ *Crossing a River*

You kneel on the verge of this impassable arroyo,
Filled now with a river instead of easy dust,
And drink it in
Literally, pumice and all, not from the sealed lips
Of your canteen but, to celebrate, from your hands,
And watch it surging
Between you and the impossible place you had meant to go,
Past a stream like a stairway, flooded and broken
At the foot of a monument
To the greater glory of stones, all cutbanks and no point bars,
A torrent not to be forded if you can't stand
The equal partnership
Of branches, rocks, and whole bushes, its leapfrogging bedload,
Which would carry you off and lose you without a murmur.
You could sit down
And eventually it would dwindle, falter, and go away
Like a second thought failing before your eyes,
Or you could climb,
Maybe, scraping your way up cliffs to its source, finding nothing,
No fountainhead to circle and mull around

Or to turn young by,
Just seasonally bad weather running off cloudy spillways.
So you head downstream on the good side of it,
Trying to get somewhere
The way it does: temporarily. This scarred, unearthly ravine
May be someone's, and the fullness thereof, but not yours,
Not even this river's
For long, as it makes up its mind about the weakness
Of what lies under it, what to carry away,
What course to choose
While glancing toward gravity, making no grand progress
And not resounding through multicolored canyons
But disappearing
Abruptly with all its rainwash in a flattening fan
In the dry silt of the playa beside you
Where, if you've played along,
You'll find your eyes intent on a different level, not broken
Yet, where water goes underground without you.
Here you are free to cross.

❧ Standing in the Middle of a Desert

You stop halfway in this bleakness to reconsider
Everything underfoot,
Which, like white sunlight and the punishing air,
Seems in favor of dying.
You don't have enough essential qualities
To vegetate here:
You may be distorted, bitter, fleshy, and smooth,
But not well armored,
Not deeply or widely rooted, gray-green, or dwarfish.
An executioner

Like that crook-backed creosote whose poisonous roots
Kill its own seedlings
(Unless some unlikely rain leaches the earth)
Has one idea: its life.
But if you stayed still and tried to be self-effacing,
You'd bear numberless offspring
Whose sincerest flattery wouldn't be imitation
But helping themselves to you:
They'd be overjoyed to live on your behalf,
Leave nothing to waste,
Leave nothing at all to your imagination,
So you have to move,
Marking your time in this intractable sand,
More footloose than ever.

❧ *At the Point of No Return*

Till now, you could have taken back your steps
Like slips of the foot:
They were turning points where, more easily than not,
You could have given up,
Gone back to the start, forgotten, tried something different.
But from here on
It will take more courage to turn than to keep going.
You take two strides,
Each boot on its own, and you're headed one way only,
Irresponsibly committed,
Refreshed by the absence of the power to choose.
You enjoy believing
Your tracks in the blowing sand (that dusty mulch
Protecting deeper water)
May offer for an hour thousands of shelters,
Small rooting places
For seeds that, without you, would have kept on tumbling

Unfulfilled downwind,
So your line of march, no matter how misdirected
By your fixed or wandering
Star-sighted, red-rimmed eyes, may be remembered
By an equally erratic,
Interrupted, and inexplicable line of survivors,
Which till their last season
Will be straining root and branch taller than dunes
To postpone their burial.

❧ *Living Off the Land*

Your eyes gnaw at the land ahead for food. You travel
Light-headed, ravenous, your jaws rehearsing
Zigzagging ruminations,
Grindings, incisive choppings, those broad-minded habits
That make you omnivorous by reputation
But in name only:
Here, in the desert, your natural disadvantages
Come into focus better than your eyes—
A rank amateur's nose,
A lack of teeth ridged well enough for the mangling of thorns,
Shortness of daily range, shortness of breath,
The griping of your guts
At the half-thought of settling for carrion like the vultures
Now effortlessly hanging fire around you,
Concerned for your welfare.
You know what coyotes know: sheep may not safely graze
With or without a shepherd near your hunger.
But being a scavenger
Means learning to skulk till carcasses and the time seem ripe.
The relative deadness of flesh depends on timing
As much as taste
Unfortunately for you, whose hungry, impatient ancestors

Survived (in a world where bones grew popular)
By being and tasting terrible:
At best, you would be last in line at communal dinners
Under this meat-loving sun, or the last of your line
At the dead head of it.
If you look under your feet, whose shrinking, hardening shadows
Match every step you take, burnt black by sunlight,
You see you could grub there
Or grovel for one more grubstake, kneeling, praying for seeds
(If any nearby have had decent burial)
To sprout and bear fruit,
But for you it's a waiting game that might take generations
To master: all the lost seasons, all the clouds
That never arrive
Except in their own good time, when you, having drifted off,
Might not remember what every seed remembers:
What it is.
You'd have turned into all you can eat, this air and this sand,
Faltering, flowing even without water
Uneventfully downwind.

✹ Reading the Landscape

You sit and breathe, scanning the raw illusions of distance
And nearness for the lay of this land, depending
On what you are,
A pivot casting the only restless shadow for miles.
Far off, the horizon traces its own downfall—
Mountainous once,
The wrack of living seas, steep fire, a storming of stones,
Now slowly settling for less under the weather,
That fearless explorer
Of weakness in the bindings of mind and matter. Nearby, lost
   ice

Through freeze and thaw has cracked a granite causeway
Where gnarled manzanita
Has made one fault its own, has wrestled for root-room,
And now bears fruit you share with unknown neighbors.
You feel strangely at home
In the visible world, a place called Here and There, on the seat
Of kings, the gluteus maximus, deluded
Into thinking you're not lost
At the heart of this bewilderment. Your only shelters
Are half-shut eyes and a shut mouth, but sand grains
(Once firm rock, now shattered)
Have entered those three rooms, sharing your misunderstandings
Of what you say and see, reminding you
Your mind's voice and mind's eye
Are equally vulnerable in their pastimes and desolations,
Their taste for all the flavors of light and shade
And the sweet nothings
Of casual, elaborate, or desperate speech. Your duties
Are to rest and be recreated, then to stand,
Ignoring all directions
But your own, and to exercise your freedom of chance by aiming
Somewhere, keeping a constant Here beside you
As faithfully as your death.

❧ Seeing Things

Browbeaten by the sun,
Squinting, and long since out of focus yourself
In a sharp-edged, keen-eyed world, you take whatever looms
Or lords it over you
Or spills its rippling lakes across this desert
More placidly than those expecting to feel cold sober.
You know that shimmer of water
Isn't for you, will keep a critical distance

Like grazing antelope sidling from your approaches.
You know that heavenly mansion
Hanging upside down or having it both ways
To a pinnacle is a shack or boulder beyond the horizon
Where you would spend hard times.
You know the delectable mountains like layer cakes
Are twice as far away as they seem and completely inedible.
But your fondness for light,
For the earth's unlimited metamorphoses,
Should help you go along with its disguises, shifting
(But not uneasily)
The burden of proof to the eyes of other beholders
Who don't know what you are, who may be seeing you now
As a menacing, blurred afrit,
A towering apparition wobbling toward them
Helplessly, their last hope, their disillusionment.

✹ Lying Awake in a Desert

Displaced by darkness, you lie flat on your back,
Putting the world behind you, and stare at the moon,
The embarrassing moon, with nothing to offer it,
No ebb or flow, no wolfish transformations
Except this lunacy you keep to yourself.

You feel defenseless at last—no choice of weapons
And no opponent, only a field of honor,
This sand where you make little or no impression,
Though it takes you as you are, dead or alive,
As a kind of minor natural disaster.

If a sound should startle you out of your unsound sleep,
Whistling, buzzing, or droning, wingbeats, scuttling
Of small dry claws, lie still. Nothing at night

Makes noise by accident. If you hear, you were meant to
Or the indifferent source has found you harmless.

No matter how cold you feel to yourself, your colleagues—
The scorpions, sidewinders, and spiny swifts—
Will come to share the benefit of your body
And its residual heat. They'll lie beside you
More trustingly than you could with a stranger.

So if you wake in the morning, do it gently,
One eye, one branch, one thought, one stretch at a time,
Being a homing place and point of departure.
Meanwhile, get through this night of reckoning
By the irrational riches of starlight.

🌿 *Looking for Water*

At the lip of your canteen, kissing that last sure drop
Goodbye, you choose the least unlikely direction—
Hills (if there are any)
Or greenness (if there is such a shade) or somewhere familiar
(If you can remember how some map unfolded
For your civilized fingers
By artificial light)—or barring those choices, anywhere.
You're keeping cool in spite of the persuasions
Of the surrounding air,
The parched ground burning underfoot, the sun too thirsty
Now that you're living by the sweat of your brow.
You watch for clouds
Like a furrow-faced, drought-plagued farmer ready to hire
The dry wits of witches, cannons of rainmakers,
Or prayers made of sand.
Though they make no streambed for that smallest of tributaries
Under your tongue, you put small stones in your mouth

For their durable comfort
But, with what remains of your breath, practice no oratory
Here in this speechless country, wasting no words
On self-absorbed cacti:
Though you behead one, crush its pale pulpy heart, squeeze out
Briefly what it had saved through fifty summers,
And leave it dying,
Your graying stubble drains off no excess heat like its needles,
And your blundering, rootless sense of territory
Can't match its self-possession.
You may find, by growing or fading light, a waterhole
With genuine liquid filling a charmed circle
Before your very knees,
But if nothing green surrounds it, one slip of the tongue,
One head-first impulse, and you may leave yourself
In a roofless mortuary,
Yet if suddenly real bushes are offering real leaves
Or if at the foot of a hill you find seep willows
Or anything blooming
In a dry creekbed or lakebed, or if you can listen hard,
Not to the ragged pulse in your mind's ear
(That deserted music)
For the actual droning of bees, for actual birdsong, and can
   follow
To the place where they've made their lives over and over,
Where deer-flies hover
Green and gold above damp sand or clay, start digging.
Wait by that emptiness. If it trickles and fills,
Your luck is only beginning.
The flies and bees will join you in that bitter communion,
Will take it with you, as drunk as true believers
Sharing another kingdom.

❧ *Getting There*

You take a final step and, look, suddenly
You're there. You've arrived
At the one place all your drudgery was aimed for:
This common ground
Where you stretch out, pressing your cheek to sandstone.
What did you want
To be? You'll remember soon. You feel like tinder
Under a burning glass,
A luminous point of change. The sky is pulsing
Against the cracked horizon,
Holding it firm till the arrival of stars
In time with your heartbeats.
Like wind etching rock, you've made a lasting impression
On the self you were
By having come all this way through all this welter
Under your own power,
Though your traces on a map would make an unpromising
Meandering lifeline.
What have you learned so far? You'll find out later,
Telling it haltingly
Like a dream, that lost traveler's dream
Under the last hill
Where through the night you'll take your time out of mind
To unburden yourself
Of elements along elementary paths
By the break of morning.
You've earned this worn-down, hard, incredible sight
Called Here and Now.
Now, what you make of it means everything,
Means starting over:
The life in your hands is neither here nor there
But getting there,
So you're standing again and breathing, beginning another
Journey without regret
Forever, being your own unpeaceable kingdom,
The end of endings.

Two

❧ *Feeding*

When I dropped bread, they swam
Out of nowhere, the fingerling
Catfish, even darker
Than the pool lying dead calm
Over them and around them.

Those inches of black ribbon
All held white crumbs like eyes
And wavered themselves away
In schools and disappeared
Again into deeper water.

When I dropped more, what came
Was an altogether stranger
Nature of moving slow,
As though the elders knew
They could be slow to swim

But would still be in time
To take what was their own
Into their own gloom
Of soft-barbed opening
And closing jaws and turn

Away in easy curves
With a sinewy suppleness,
Undulant, fading down
To what they might become
Somewhere still more dim.

When I broke the final crust,
What rose to the underface
Of the pond (so slow, it seemed
Too slow to lift a form
That huge from so far under)

Has kept its place in the night
Of my mind since I was four,
Moving its perfectly sure,
Unhurried, widening mouth
Toward whiteness to darken it.

⚜ The Truant Officer's Helper

My only day in the black
Old truant officer's truck,
Grandfather and I
Went lurching and jouncing
Over raw country roads
To find boys playing hooky.
Their mothers on sagging porches
With steel-gray hair coming down
The sides of their sad faces
Would say they didn't know
What their boys were up to
Or where in the world they were,
But my grandfather knew.

His voice as calm and soft
And sure as during grace,
He told their mothers on them:
They were fishing in Sippo Creek
Or fighting in alleys
Or playing with guinea pigs
In back of the hospital
Or sniping butts in gutters
Or swimming and taking leaks
In the town's pure drinking water,
Not listening to their teachers,
Not learning their three Rs.

Bad boys stayed out of school
With no excuse from doctors
Or mothers, dentists or fathers.
We hunted them everywhere:
In orchards and vacant lots,
In carbarns and pool halls
And down by the canal
Where bums held their own classes,
All those tempting places

I might have gone myself
If I'd been old
Or bad or brave enough.

By afternoon we'd caught
Only one guilty sinner
Red-handed with swiped berries,
Red hair still wet,
A trespassing skinny-dipper
From out at the gravel pit,
And we brought him back alive
To Henry Wadsworth Longfellow
Junior High School, hanging
His head. Grandfather told him
Never to yield to temptation,
Never to steal or tell stories,
To grow up good and smart
As a Presbyterian,
Then sent him to his Doom.

My mother knew where *I* was
And gave me a good excuse:
I was helping my grandfather
Find bad boys and refill
The shelves of a magic storehouse,
A cave of Ali Baba,
With jars of paste and notebooks
And chalk and bottles of ink
And rubber stamps and rulers.
Longfellow over the door
Told us the thoughts of youth
Were long, long thoughts, but mine
In that dim supply room
Were short as my light fingers.

That night in a shed loft
I flew with a featherbed
By lamplight, writing my first
Short story full of lies
About a secret country
And a boy who disobeyed
And ran away in a dream.
I tried hard to be good
And smart and made it up
Out of my own head
On that stolen paper,
My stolen pencil trembling.

✤ *My Pets*

I had none in our house
And none in our back yard,
But one morning I found them
Down the red sandstone alley
Waiting against the wall
At the foot of the hospital.

They crouched in chicken crates
Stacked wobbly: calico
And piebald lumps with no tails
Or ears, almost no mouths
Till I poked in stems of hay
And suddenly the fur

Came open under their noses,
And they browsed out of my hands.
I had fed myself for years
But never anything else
So hungry. They knew how
To sing for their dry suppers.

When the old man gave them water
They whistled like cardinals,
But struggled to get loose
If he held them. We had too many
Mouths at our house already,
Our father said after grace.

For a week I watched them go
Squirming, one at a time,
Half-whistling and half-squealing
In the old man's careful gloves
Through the delivery door
Before I could give them names.

❧ Our Father

He held so much
Anger in him quiet
Heavy nobody
Had ever hit him
Once he never had to
Hit anybody either
But would just look
Hard in the face
Those hands that flat
Belly it was over
Before any slap back talk
Could start our father
Snored through the wall
So loud beside us
We could still hear
Him in the morning
When he was gone
To work in the rumble
Screech clank slam
Of the rusty steelmill
That made him all week
Too tired too far
Away burned up
Burned out to talk too hard
Of hearing to please
He would try to
Listen sometimes glaring
At our mouths asking
What he would say what
Did you say what was it
Too hard to say it
Loud if we were scared
If we mumbled whatever
We could never shout
What we wanted to keep
Quiet my older brother

The star outfielder the star
Center the scholar I wanted
To be lost
Sleep in that room
In that bed beside me
He told our mother
He felt afraid
In the night all night
Long I was dead
He would say David
Listening hard to hear
Me breathe just once to see
Me move my mouth
My body that could run
Like his so far so loud
All day so tired wake up
He would say please over
And over shaking.

❧ Boy Jesus

When they made me the boy Jesus
In the Sunday school Christmas pageant, oh Jesus,
I would have given almost anything
To be anybody else in the world but a made-up Jesus.

But suddenly it was too late to say anything
Polite against it or do anything
Desperate in my knee-length toga, while my squirming friends
Snickered in the pews, or even *feel* anything

As I floated down the endless aisle, praying those friends
Would forget someday and be real friends
And not remember me forever singing that damned song
In a shaky soprano, "All Men Be Loving Friends."

It would have been terrible enough singing any song
In public, even the school fight song,
But to have to look so holy-faced and fluttery while I,
Of all young sinners, sang it, made it my swan song.

Why had they picked on me? Jesus and I
Gave each other a pain: I couldn't stump preachers, could I?
No dove had come flapping down when I was baptized, I was
    no boy
Genius, and we were Laurel and Hardy carpenters, my father
    and I.

And my voice was breaking: I was only half a boy,
A sneak-thief, liar, prober of loveless keyholes, a would-be boy
Magician, a card-stacker more ruled by swear-words
Than by Jesus Christ Almighty, the Good Boy.

From that day on, I put my fidgety faith in my own words
And later in love—in ugly, profane, beautiful words,
Instead of going hook, line, and sinker for Jesus—
No Gospels for the Fishers of Men, but love in other words.

🌿 *The Junior High School Band Concert*

When our semi-conductor
Raised his baton, we sat there
Gaping at *Marche Militaire,*
Our mouth-opening number.
It seemed faintly familiar
(We'd rehearsed it all that winter),
But we attacked in such a blur,
No army anywhere
On its stomach or all fours
Could have squeezed through our crossfire.

I played cornet, seventh chair
Out of seven, my embouchure
A glorified Bronx cheer
Through that three-keyed keyhole stopper
And neighborhood window-slammer
Where mildew fought for air
At every exhausted corner,
My fingering still unsure
After scaling it for a year
Except on the spit-valve lever.

Each straight-faced mother and father
Retested his moral fiber
Against our traps and slurs
And the inadvertent whickers
Paradiddled by our snares,
And when the brass bulled forth
A blare fit to horn over
Jericho two bars sooner
Than Joshua's harsh measures,
They still had the nerve to stare.

By the last lost chord, our director
Looked older and soberer.
No doubt, in his mind's ear

Some band somewhere
In some Music of some Sphere
Was striking a note as pure
As the wishes of Franz Schubert,
But meanwhile here we were:
A lesson in everything minor,
Decomposing our first composer.

❧ *Jeremiad*

The night I was Jeremiah
In the Sunday school panorama
Unraveling the Bible
From Exodus to Easter,
The Word of the Lord came unto me (memorized
In a cold garage
With no help from our Chrysler):
I was announcing Woe
Between Gary and Chicago
Where it was wonderful shouting
We could all be wiped out clean
By God some smoky morning.

The beard of this prophet
Was a black-crape botch-up
Whose gum had just enough spirit
To lose its place in the windy
Word of the Lord coming out of me slightly garbled
To tell those rows of pews
They'd be exceedingly massacred
While my robe of miscast curtains
Puffed dust into my ears,
A warning cloud from the wilderness
Of our attic, a parable
As dry as Israel's cisterns.

Isaiah softened them up
And then I let them have it,
And not even sweet Jesus
Who came on later could flatten
The Word of the Lord we'd rammed in first and loudest.
Since our feet didn't show,
All of us wise old prophets
Wore sneakers and sneaked out

Before the Crucifixion,
Still full of lost diatribes
As the Golden Rule's star turn
Ran smack into our Doomsday.

❧ *My Father's Garden*

On his way to the open hearth where white-hot steel
Boiled against furnace walls in wait for his lance
To pierce the fireclay and set loose demons
And dragons in molten tons, blazing
Down to the huge satanic caldrons,
Each day he would pass the scrapyard, his kind of garden.

In rusty rockeries of stoves and brake drums,
In grottoes of sewing machines and refrigerators,
He would pick flowers for us: small gears and cogwheels
With teeth like petals, with holes for anthers,
Long stalks of lead to be poured into toy soldiers,
Ball bearings as big as grapes to knock them down.

He was called a melter. He tried to keep his brain
From melting in those tyger-mouthed mills
Where the same steel reappeared over and over
To be reborn in the fire as something better
Or worse: cannons or cars, needles or girders,
Flagpoles, swords, or plowshares.

But it melted. His classical learning ran
Down and away from him, not burning bright.
His fingers culled a few cold scraps of Latin
And Greek, *magna sine laude,* for crosswords
And brought home lumps of tin and sewer grills
As if they were his ripe prize vegetables.

✤ My Fire

In the cave under our house
I tended the fire: a furnace
Where black fossils of ferns
And swamp-shaking dinosaurs
Would burn through the cold mornings
If I shook the dying and dead
Ashes down through the grate
And, with firetongs, hauled out clinkers
Like the vertebrae of monsters.

I made my magic there,
Not the bloody charms of hunters,
Not shamans or animals
Painted on damp walls,
But something from fire. My father
Tended huge rows of fires
And burned with them all day,
Sometimes all evening, all night
In a steelmill, brought fire home
On his face and his burnt skin
And slept, glowing dark red.

My fire made steam in coils
And pipes and radiators
Poured from the steel he made
Somewhere I'd only seen
Far off, the burning mountains
Where God kept His true flame
To Himself, melting and turning
Blood-colored ore to pigs
And men to something stranger.

My spirit would swell and sing
Inside those pipes, would knock
And rattle to be let out,
Would circle through walls and floors,

Turn back to water and fall
To the fire again, turn white,
Rise hissing in every room
Against the windows to grow
Fronds and bone-white flowers,
All ice in a frozen garden.

❧ My Father's Wall

The old one was falling: the cracked gravelly pieces flaking
Like a good start on a ruin down the steep driveway
Into our basement garage. My father (stonemason
Self-taught) and I (apprentice to other sorcerers)
Slapped up the shiplap form with soleplates and raking shores
Sawed out of foundling lumber. When the truck backed in
With two yards of ready-mix jumbling in its drum
And the chute swung over, we thought we'd be all set.

The bulges started low—planks springing out like strakes
And a gray mass surging and slobbering at our ankles—
And as he braced and yelled and improvised, I shoveled
What leaked below back over that unmanned barricade
Again and again, but it flushed down through six feet of baffles
Faster than I could keep it up. I'd shoveled coal and cinders,
Sand and dirt, even manure in my meager time, but nothing
That had wanted to be somewhere else and something else so
    badly.

Gradually the mess thickened and slowed, and more stayed in
Than ran away. It put up with our planks, now only dripping
Through the sprung seams, and while our overalls hardened
Into permanent contortions like war-memorial drapery
And our feet grew heavier inside their concrete boots,
We left it to bleed all night without us. But in my sleep
I listened for all four tons to break loose, rumbling downslope
To the garage, a solid, no-nonsense, no-passenger family tank.

❧ My Physics Teacher

He tried to convince us, but his billiard ball
Fell faster than his Ping-Pong ball and thumped
To the floor first, in spite of Galileo.
The rainbows from his prism skidded off-screen
Before we could tell an infra from an ultra.
His hand-cranked generator refused to spit
Sparks and settled for smoke. The dangling pith
Ignored the attractions of his amber wand,
No matter how much static he rubbed and dubbed
From the seat of his pants, and the housebrick
He lowered into a tub of water lost
More weight (Eureka!) than the overflow.

He believed in a World of Laws, where problems had answers,
Where tangible objects and intangible forces
Acting thereon could be lettered, numbered, and crammed
Through our tough skulls for lifetimes of homework.
But his only uncontestable demonstration
Came with our last class: he broke his chalk
On a formula, stooped to catch it, knocked his forehead
On the eraser-gutter, staggered slewfoot, and stuck
One foot forever into the wastebasket.

❧ Coming Home Late with the Bad Young Man

So many tangled feet from home among toads
No bigger than june bugs hopping at mosquitoes
Dizzily we could keep our head while all
About us the wobbly sprinklers were losing theirs
To the night over lawns like upside-down chandeliers
Along the sidewalk to make it glassy-eyed
To the steps not stopping soaked on the front porch
With the right key in our hand held wrong side up
The first try under the gasp of the screendoor stopper
As soft as the click of the nightlatch being good
At keeping strictly quiet the bad young man
Amounting to nothing risking hell tiptoeing
Sockfoot along our hallway breathless with beer
To squeak the floor in time with our father's snoring
But caught in the act between dull saws out of step
By our mother's forgiving unforgetful ears
In the darkness arms outstretched for the sneaky brother
Who lived inside our head not saying prayers
Not thinking purely of girls who believed in virgins
Tomcatting out to lead us gladly astray
To show us the way to go home to let us down
On our bed who didn't brush our teeth not washing
The lipstick off our face who couldn't find
Our pajamas with all four hands who lay there staring
Like a mind's eye groggily dimly at the ceiling
As we turned to fall disgraced into the morning.

❧ *The Best Slow Dancer*

Under the sagging clotheslines of crepe paper
By the second string of teachers and wallflowers
In the school gym across the key through the glitter
Of mirrored light three-second rule forever
Suspended you danced with her the best slow dancer
Who stood on tiptoe who almost wasn't there
In your arms like music she knew just how to answer
The question mark of your spine your hand in hers
The other touching that place between her shoulders
Trembling your countless feet light-footed sure
To move as they wished wherever you might stagger
Without her she turned in time she knew where you were
In time she turned her body into yours
As you moved from thigh to secrets to breast yet never
Where you would be for all time never closer
Than your cheek against her temple her ear just under
Your lips that tried all evening long to tell her
You weren't the worst one not the boy whose mother
Had taught him to count to murmur over and over
One slide two slide three slide now no longer
The one in the hallway after class the scuffler
The double clubfoot gawker the mouth breather
With the wrong haircut who would never kiss her
But see her dancing off with someone or other
Older more clever smoother dreamier
Not waving a sister somebody else's partner
Lover while you went floating home through the air
To lie down lighter than air in a moonlit shimmer
Alone to whisper yourself to sleep remember.

After the High School Graduation, 1944

Who was I over the top
Rung of the ladder leading
Nowhere but up up
Into the night declaiming
Out of the wonder
Of original whiskey
My first glass first class first
Prize speech to the ranks
Of houses emptied
Of their sons in the dark is life
So dear or peace so sweet oh
Patrick Henry rousing
My carousing classmates
Ghostly below me leaping
The sawhorse staggering
Through zigzag rails
To crawl to the swinging bars
And the mudpit galloping
Together they thought now
Forever over the playground
Rebuilt for the building
Of our bodies' marvelous war
With each other as we were
What we were starlit performers
Reconquering all
Obstacles where what it was
That gentlemen wished
What they would have
For graduation was the gift
Of my voice making the most
Of treason by exercising
The clash of resounding arms
Around legs and bodies no longer
School spirited away
By teachers but by a primed

Loaded good cheerleading
Petty class officer
Me with the last word
On the subject of the unknown
Sheepskinned soldiers not death
That night but liberty.

✢ *The Track Scale Weigher*

Out of the blackened mouth
Of the steelmill, ingots came
On flatcars, huge and glowing
From open-hearth crucibles
But dying from white to scarlet
To maroon in the black rain
Where suddenly they scattered
Their sparks like starbursts
Of shellfire or lightning strokes
Through the ashes of twilight.

I had to weigh those gods
On a scale in deadweight tons
Alone in a small cell
At night, where the blast of their heat
Through steam and safety glass
And firebrick against my skin
Withered me, forced me to turn
Away in awe and fear.

My father had fed the fire
Where they were born, had melted
And fused them slowly
Under his hard eye
And the judgment of his masters
From wreckage and iron ore,
Alloys and mysteries,
Had poured them into forms
That could shake the earth
Under me and did
As they passed by, still burning.

That earth was newly made
And newly left for dead,
Pounded and pile-driven
To an escape-proof island

Impossible to tunnel
On the shore of a dead lake
Not by creators of worlds
But makers of cinders,
Cremators of dead gods
And fathers, surrounded
By darkness and barbed-wire.

I walked on it one midnight
Through death by air, through death
By fire, through death by water
And earth where nothing grew
Under a searchlit glare
And a starless overcast
From the smoke of furnaces
Under my father's care
Past the guards at the gate
And their cold case-hardened faces,
And finally out from under
Old orders I walked away,
Tearing my number off,
Not daring to look back.

Looking for Nellie Washington

My job in a hard time
Was to bring those people down
To the small loan man
For a mouth-to-mouth discussion
When they'd fallen far behind
Like Nellie Washington
Who lived up a street across
An alley at the top
Of a crooked stairway through
A fence in a side yard
High-stepping down concrete
To a drain behind a basement
Garage you know by the cans
Against the incinerator.

When I finally seemed to be
Somewhere I asked somebody
Or other whereabouts
Is Nellie Washington living
Somehow around near dark
Any more the manager
Would dearly like to see her
Immediately at the latest
Or at least sooner
To talk if possible
In person the whole thing over
On the telephone tomorrow.

Then nobody I could name
Would say she headed south
Or north to a neighborhood
Next door to a home far away
In bed going to work
In school after the wreck
On the road to the hospital
Except for an hour ago

Yesterday just last week
She was downstairs in the front
Of the back in number something
As far as they could forget
To say what she looked like.

In back of the front I almost
Saw through a crack in a door
A shape moving beyond
A strip of stained wallpaper
Banana-peeled to the floor
Like a windowshade unwound
To the edge of a curled carpet
Something maybe like her
One black hand turned light
At the frame to flip goodbye
A moment before it faded
Away shut gone for good
Forever like her credit.

Does her bad-account-chaser's card
Wherever it went still say
Nothing Nothing Nobody
Called Called Again Nellie
Washington where are you now
That your better business number
Was up to be disconnected
Down in black against white
On the dotted line of the Man
When you didn't come on in
Come out wherever you were
Supreme as mysterious
Unlimited beyond me
As God the National Debt
With interest so long forgiven
As I owe you I quit.

❧ *My Father in the Basement*

Something had gone wrong down in the basement.
Something important needed rearranging
Or shaping up down there like the neat shadows
He kept in the coal bin and under the workbench.
But when he went to find it, he couldn't find it.

None of the fuses had blown as dark as storms
At their tiny portholes. Nothing was on fire
But the fire in the furnace, and nothing was frozen
But the humming freezer and the concrete floor
And the hands he'd poured it with, now cold and hard.

Had his mother sent him there to fetch crab apples,
Spicy and gold, or piccalilli for supper?
Was that his father shouting and then turning
A deaf ear to his answer? It was cold
And hard to remember why he wasn't working.

So he lay down on the floor, doing things right
The first time because nothing was worth doing
Unless he did it himself. There was no use
In calling strangers if something was out of order
Because if he couldn't fix it, nobody could.

❧ My Father's Football Game

He watched each TV game for all he was worth, while swaying
Off guard or around end, his jaw
Off center. He made each tackle
Personally, took it personally if the runner broke through
To a broken field. He wanted that hotshot
Down, up and around and down
Hard, on the ground, now, no matter which team was which.

Star backs got all the cheers. Their names came rumbling,
    roaring
Out of grandstands from the loud mouths
Of their fathers. He'd show them
How it felt out cold for a loss, to be speared, the pigskin
Fumbled and turned over. Man
To man he would smile then
For the linemen, *his* team, the scoreless iron men getting even.

But if those flashy legs went flickering out of the clutches
Of the last tackler into the open
Past anyone's goal line, he would stand
For a moment of silence, bent, then take his bitter cup
To the kitchen, knowing time
Had been called for something sweeter
Than any victory: he would settle down to his dream game

Against Jim Thorpe and the Carlisle Indians for Washington
& Jefferson, buddy, that Great Year
By George Nineteen Sixteen
In mud, sweat, and sleet, in padding thinner than chain mail,
With immortal guts and helmets
Flying, the Savages versus the Heroes
By failing light in a *Götterdämmerung,* Nothing to Nothing.

❧ *The Play*

Crouching, he was falling
Forward suddenly the way
A lineman should go
At the snap from center:
Headlong but holding
His same position
Against all interference,
All trick shifts, his weight
Overbalanced heavily
Toward what came rushing
Against him, that carrier,
That wingback. We lifted him
Clumsily halfway under
The slump of the shoulders,
His shape so solid now,
So gray, we could hardly
Budge him. He thought
He had to be there
With his whole body
To defend his territory,
Arms locked so no one
Could get through
Without his say-so.
He was still
In the game, a part
Of the action, the team player,
The loyal tackler, rock-sure
Through all those losing seasons
Believing he was the key
To every play though never
More than one more number
To the real playmaker.
Exit on a stretcher
The heavy father.

❧ My Father's Ghost

If you count nine stars and nine stones, then look into
an empty room, you'll see a ghost.
—Midwestern Folk Belief

I counted them, and now I look through the door
Into the empty room where he was, where nine stars
Have failed to conjure him under a ceiling
Presiding over nothing except a floor
And four walls without windows, where nine stones
Have failed to call him up from the netherworld
To tell me of his cruel unnatural murder.

He stays as invisible as other souls
In either world. I have to imagine him
In this interior without natural light,
Recall him burned by splashing steel each shift
Of his unnatural life, his thigh broken
To an Oedipal limp, his eyes half-blinded
By staring into the pits of open hearths,
His memory put to sleep, his ears deafened
By the slamming of drop forges and the roar
Of fire as bright as the terrible hearts of stars,
Of fire that would melt stones. He won't come back
At anyone's bidding in his hard hat of a helmet,
His goggles up like a visor, but I dream him
Returning unarmed, unharmed. Words, words. I hold
My father's ghost in my arms in his dark doorway.

✤ *Elegy for My Mother*

She heard the least footfall, the least sigh
Or whisper beyond a door, the turning
Of a page in a far room, the most distant birdsong,

Even a slight wind when it was barely
Beginning: she would wait at a window
For someone to come home, for someone sleeping

To stir and waken, for someone far away
To tell her anything she could murmur
Word for word for years, for those close by

To be alive and well in stories she loved
To listen to all day, where life after life
Kept happening to others, but not to her,

And it was no surprise to forget herself
One morning, to misplace wherever she was,
Whoever she was, and become a ghostly wonder

Who would never wonder why it didn't matter
If no one listened to her or whether
She was here or there or even somewhere

Or why it felt so easy not to linger
In the doorway saying hello, goodbye, or remember
Me, but simply to turn and disappear.

❧ Songs My Mother Taught Me

In a small throaty soprano
In perfect pitch always,
She sang "Thou Art Repose"
Before my feet could touch
The floor from the music bench
And "The Trout"—Schubert at peace
With his mildest remembrance,
Then glittering with fear.
I remember listening, awed
That her fingers touching the keys
(Too small to reach octaves)

Could clear a way for her voice
To stream through such music
Composed by real composers
Who had used just pen and ink
(A skill I'd halfway mastered
By scrawling words, not notes),
All dead, all living again
Each time she played and sang
"On Wings of Song," "Pale Hands
I Loved," *"Ich liebe dich,"*
"None but the Lonely Heart."

Now like Franz and Felix,
Amy, Edvard, and Piotr,
She depends on someone else
To sing what she dreamed of.
She has gone to her long rest
By the restless, restful waters
Of whatever Shalimar
Or Ganges she longed for
In Zeit und Ewigkeit,
Her heart no longer lonely,
And I sing this for her.

✣ In the Dream House

My father, having changed
From his comfortable well-worn
Once-in-a-lifetime tweeds,
Which he never owned, wears now
As the man of the dream house
A flower in his silk lapel
And stands poised by my mother
Who is radiantly younger
In the dress he never bought her
And kisses her longingly
And lingeringly, not fearful
Of heaven or the neighbors,
As if he'd loved her before
The taxi, the orchestra,
The champagne, and the private laughter,
Which they never called or heard
Or opened or uttered,
And they're holding each other
Not with self-contained arms
But with one accord, one impulse
Of uncontrollable joy
Over what could be their lives,
And there in his firelit den
He looks at her and smiles
Out of pride with open eyes,
Which he no longer has.

❧ Their Bodies

to the students of anatomy at Indiana University

That gaunt old man came first, his hair as white
As your scoured tables. Maybe you'll recollect him
By the scars of steel-mill burns on the backs of his hands,
On the nape of his neck, on his arms and sinewy legs,
And her by the enduring innocence
Of her face, as open to all of you in death
As it would have been in life: she would memorize
Your names and ages and pastimes and hometowns
If she could, but she can't now, so remember her.

They believed in doctors, listened to their advice,
And followed it faithfully. You should treat them
One last time as they would have treated you.
They had been kind to others all their lives
And believed in being useful. Remember somewhere
Their son is trying hard to believe you'll learn
As much as possible from them, as *he* did,
And will do your best to learn politely and truly.

They gave away the gift of those useful bodies
Against his wish. (They had their own ways
Of doing everything, always.) If you're not certain
Which ones are theirs, be gentle to everybody.

Sequence: The Land Behind the Wind

❧

❧ Making Camp

When their eyes opened, it was more than morning.
They lay by a fallen tree as if it had burned
All night for them, a backlog
Where the true burning came from red crest lichen
And the green blaze of star moss.
There was no other fire except among leaves
Overhead, among leaves beside them.

They had changed. They had been changed. They saw
As clearly as if the air had turned to light
Spineleaf moss and earthstar
Without moving their hands or their bodies,
Map lichen gleaming on rock, not saying where
They were, not saying where to go,
But to begin.

They began making their camp crosswind by water
Facing the southerly bent firebow
Of the sun. They gathered the dead
Branches that had kept the sky from falling
Before falling themselves.
They gathered boughs, a browse bed and a firebed
And, at the turning point, made fire.

❧ *Their Fire*

Their fire was small. They fed it only enough
To keep it through the night and to keep them
Together and unafraid
Lying between it and the face of the cliff
Where, at the foot under a hanging stone,
They had made their shelter
For a time, as others had in years so distant
Now, they seemed as thick and soft as the stillness
Standing around their sleep
In which the animals also slept (the beavers
And otters whose doors were deep under the water,
Squirrels in their hollows)
Or walked in the sleep of others (the gray foxes,
The martens and black bears, silent, listening).
Had they too wondered,
Those other makers of fire, how long to linger
In this same place, how many living seasons
It would keep them warm,
Would hold them together at a single hearthstone
While the round year turned the sky, thickened the clouds
Or thinned them, turning
The snow and the rain as it turned the wind, turned leaves
And turned the color of their hair like ermine's fur

And turned the earth?
They held their hands out to that restless fire
As if to shield it, to calm it, and they turned
Their faces into its light.

❧ *Their Shelter*

They sheltered under a spruce in the sudden storm,
At its foot layered the soft boughs
Of a browse bed and then lay down while rain
And snow mingled along the branches
Above them, around them, in a blue-green darkness.

The tree was their house, its trunk their lodgepole,
A single wall spreading its pungent needles
To waver over their half-sleep, their rooftree
With down-swept rafters whispering
As high as they could hear and far underground.

It spoke all night to them out of the earth,
Out of the sky. It said *the rain,* said *wind,*
Said *snow and ice,* and *deep* and *here.* Their hearts
Were drumming against the night like the wings of grouse.
Their only fire was their hearts against the night.

❧ *Backtracking*

Finding the right way back seemed easy at first:
By glancing aside
At the blazes they'd left only a day ago
(Still bleeding, still white

Even in darkness), they followed their own trail
Through the forest, recalling
Exactly, easily how not to be sidetracked
Where their feet had veered
Before on other paths, at the beckoning
Of the startled and startling
Outcries of birds, moth-flight, the dim retreats
Of wood fern and adder's-tongue.
They knew where they were: where they had been before,
Where they had found nothing
To fear, where all they had to do was remember
To take each step
Back by reflecting, and they would find themselves
Again where they'd started.
But gradually by day and gradual evening
The footprints grew fainter.
The leaves had recovered from their careless passage.
The grass had turned
Upright and smooth, no longer bending toward them
In their old direction,
And the bare ground had leveled away their traces
Like snow melting.
They were uncertain whether the marks were theirs
Or from hooves or paws
Or the gouges of fallen branches already gone
Crosspath to earth.
Were those their blazes now or natural scars
Aging and hardening
Over the knots they crowned against hard winter?
How could they know
They were finding their own way back, not someone else's,
Not some stranger's
Who'd been blind-canyoned, who'd blundered out of nowhere
Or into it? There was no way
To tell any longer whether the signs they saw
Underfoot or felt with their fingers

Had been coming or going, whether the ones who'd made them
Were living or dead
Or had turned into the light of a lost clearing
Where everything had begun
And might begin again. They kept on walking,
Dreaming they were there.

⚘ *His Dream*

He catches sight of it, finally, in the distance:
The house he had tried so hard to remember
Day after footsore day when, stumbling
Under the burden of sunlight, he had stared
Up canyons, down weathered valleys, only to find
An emptiness once more, a perfectly
Beautiful and beckoning emptiness
Toward which he would stride willingly
And willfully, pacing himself till sundown.

He'd known he would recognize it without knowing
Whether its windows were glass or simply holes,
Whether its roof was slanted and firm—or missing.
He sees someone has lived there, surrounding it
With trees that had once been wild, with wildflowers,
Has smoothed its yard, has cornered and folded down
Grass-beds, has bedded fragments of stone
So feet can find their preordained directions,
Has numbered the lintel, has left the door ajar.

He moves toward it, sleepwalking easily
Over the easy earth, and it lets him in.
What are these rooms? Why are so many walls
Standing unchangeably upright around him?
Why do the floors and ceilings end in corners?

What is there here for him? Nothing remains,
Nothing he wants as deeply as what he's found
Outside of houses, no feeling as full of wonder
As being tired and restless, eager and lost.

And now he dreams he has finished dreaming. His body
Is lying under the pale rooftree of morning,
Under a movable and changeable sky,
And for a moment, only a moment,
He reaches the right true end of traveling,
A place to be still, a place to belong in,
Where forgetting to be himself is the final
Incredible comfort he had always forgotten
Even to wish for. He stands and goes on walking.

❧ *Her Dream and the Awakening*

She had become a tree, and two dark birds
Had built their nest in her, had woven
Moss and dead grass
Into a shape no larger than cupped hands
Where now a single egg was gleaming
Like a blackened moon
In the cup of a half-sky, both newly broken
Out of the night. She was in the earth
And above it, and all weather
Was hers alone now. Nothing could fall
That had not already fallen. The birds within her
Sang their first song: silence. Then she saw
Near the ground, making its own small fire,
The woodsman's glistening ax.

She woke in pain. She was lying where she had fallen,
And her mouth was frozen.
Nothing would come from it. Her eyes would not
Open. Had she been thrown down
To this hard ground she could feel
With both her hands? Or had she really chosen
To touch it with so much of her body
At once and yielded her sense of direction
To the long-drawn unrelenting mothering
Call of the earth? The pain was in her heart,
The dungeon at the heart of her rib-caged center
Of balance now telling her it had lost its hold
On her dancing master.
The pain was telling her she was no longer
Held on strings leading up through the dark sky
To those great careless fingers. She heard singing.
Slowly she sat up, and her eyes opened
By themselves. She was in a forest. It was morning.
The woodsman had not killed her. She was flesh
And bone, and the pain was fading
Like all her memories of the terrible palace.
Wild birds and animals had gathered around her,
Looking into her eyes, watching and waiting.

❧ *The Source*

Neither had said they were going to climb to it,
But they kept walking beside the stream
Under the high shade
Of fir trees, upslope, wading through ferns and leaves
As if through a living and dying current,
Through water itself
Whenever the sea-green walls of the creek bank
Steepened to overhangs where roots

Clung wrong-side up
And seedling firs lurched out from under a world
That dared them to survive one birth.
They shared smooth stones
With sandpipers and dippers, with gold-eyed frogs,
Shared low-slung branches with green herons,
With kingfishers,
Warblers, and winter wrens, who watched them pass
Songless to higher ground, to a light
Thinning out, a waterfall
Where the creek was rain and a sideways mist and past
The sidelong mouths of runnels and freshets
Glistening, as cold
To their fingers' touch as the promises of winter.
More shallow, its stones no longer softened
By white-water crowfoot and pale
Flowerless fountain moss, the creek seemed younger,
Hurrying, its surface quick, more hectic,
As if it felt no longing
Yet to have anything like the sea to turn to.
They climbed past thicker and smaller trees,
Past the half-dead
And the weathered barkless gray dead at the treeline,
Climbed toward spillways of snow on the mountain
Through avalanche lily, sorrel,
Through lupine, through snow, the light a snowfall,
A blue-white daylight the color of snowmelt
Shimmering by their feet,
Still only half persuaded not to be ice
But to give in to the full beginning
Of flowing. At the rim
Of a pond near the foot of steep snow-drifted talus,
Half-frozen, they knelt where the foot-wide creek
Was now being born
Again and again under their eyes. They drank
From the source, their blue lips going numb

At that strange kiss.
They kissed like strangers. They watched the creek spill over
Stones like first words: *Only
Begin, and the rest will follow.*

❧ *Seeing the Wind*

Long ago, they had tasted a wind like milk. It was still
On their tongues, a claim against earth, and they turned now
In the quiet air and waited for that wind
To come to the horizon. They knew they would know
Its beginning far off, its moving face
Bending the distant grass-heads and tree crowns
Before it, its shape a storm cloud falling forward
To find them. This time, they would welcome it.

They wouldn't find it strange. It had a name
Drawn from its birthplace, not from where it was
At the moment of meeting, not from where it was going
To die. They knew that name, and they saw it
Begin then, coming toward them. They held their eyes
Open to know it, arms open to take it in
Where it belonged, in their bones, not only blowing
Among them as it might through their skeletons

If they lay down, but inside their hollows, a marrow
Like the music of their blood being reborn
Over and over. It came toward their bodies
As they faced into it, becoming what filled them
As the wind became what filled it, what it moved,
And what moved it, and they watched it passing
Through all they knew, through all they had ever known,
Through all they would know tomorrow of love and fear.

❧ *Walking into the Wind*

After walking into the wind all day, they would rest
Beneath it in the open night, while it murmured
The promises and taunts of a restless lover.
Though they knew where they might shelter, warming their
   hearts
Among trees and houses, no longer listening
To anything at all in the darkness,
They slept instead where it could touch them
And touch them with its fingers till morning.

They would wake to its whisper then and stand
To face it. Though it veered to a different quarter
Or baffled them, gusting and pausing, dying,
Shifting their landmarks, they would go on walking
Toward it, toward its source. They had known the Country
Of the Blind and the Fortunate Isles by the lovely
Bitter hearsay of elders and lying strangers,
But they dreamed of a place to stand behind the wind.

Before they had faltered to their knees, they found it:
The air fell still, the horizon drew in close,
Binding them in cold arms. Held them turning
Slowly. Encircled them. They turned in circles
As predictably as all lost travelers
Finding no help in any direction, moving
But motionless, holding their bare ground.
There lay the wind at their feet like a pathway.

Three

❧ Stump Speech

This is the bark, which is always dead.

This is the phloem, which only lives
To carry sunlight down from the leaves,
Then dies into bark, which is always dead.

This is the cambium. Every year
It thickens another ring to wear
And swells the phloem, which only lives
To carry sunlight down from the leaves,
Then dies into bark, which is always dead.

This is the xylem. It lifts the rain
Two hundred feet from root to vein
Out of a cambium well. Each year
It thickens another ring to wear
And swells the phloem, which only lives
To carry sunlight down from the leaves,
Then dies into bark, which is always dead.

This is the heartwood, once locked in
As hard as iron by pitch and resin
Inside the xylem that lifted rain
Two hundred feet from root to vein,
Now soft as cambium out to where
It thickened a final ring to wear,
Then shrank like the phloem that swelled with life
Called down like sunlight from each leaf
Behind the bark, which is always dead.

And this is the stump I stand beside,
Once tall, now short as the day it died
And gray as driftwood, its heartwood eaten
By years of weather, its xylem rotten
And only able to hold the rain
One cold inch (roots withered and gone)

In a shallow basin, a cracked urn
Whose cambium and phloem now learn
To carry nothing down to the dark
Inside the broken shell of the bark
But a dream of a tree forever dead.

And this is the speech that grew instead.

✣ *Looking into a Pond*

The leaves have floated across the shallow pond
For days, yellow but darkening, and now
They fall a second time to the mud below

Where I see them lie like water churned by a storm,
The stems and the cupped blades nesting together,
Not moving, turning green again beneath algae

And moldering under silt that will smooth them slowly
Away under the underface where air
And water touch, where still another surface

Comes down now at a slant to take my eyes:
The birdless, cloud-bearing, endless, cold, and coldly
Reflected sky where air and nothing meet.

❧ *Algae*

They are floating, suspended
In the still pondwater
Under the touching, the rippling
Of water striders, the hovering
Sheen of damselflies, not needing
To care where wind and sun
Are going, but drifting
Rootless and leafless, flowerless,
Their green translucent hair-thin
Bodies feeding and turning
On the long threads of daylight.

Now at the edging-over
Of winter, the first fall
Of whiteness, they settle
Downward, they soften, they gather
To rest, they darken
For a dark season, waiting
To lift new lives to their sky-pale
Likeness, to rise gently,
To mirror the spring rain.

❧ *The Water Lily*

As slowly, as carefully as a wading bird
The elderly Japanese photographer
Comes down stone steps under leaves through pale-green light
To the pond and wavers
At the brink where a single water lily
White around gold lies open. Bending, he stares
Long and, bending farther, moves
Along the bankside, pauses again to gaze,
To focus at last, to shift, to hesitate,
To lift his eyes among wrinkles, to lift one shoulder
And one slow corner of his mouth, to take no picture
But slowly to turn away,
To take nothing away but his mind's eye.

Our Model

By the forest pond while I sit watching
Under the maples, she makes up her features
In a compact mirror for a photographer,
Already a picture in pale green and rose.

When he points to a green ledge, she tiptoes there
Unsteadily on high heels, lifting aside
The ferns with her fingernails, bends down to feel
A fabric-sample of moss, then seats herself.

Undisturbed by birdsong, she begins posing,
Tilting her face in profile, then suddenly
Confronting the lens wide-eyed. The air-soft swirl
Of her hair comes sweeping darkly along her cheekbones.

Again and again she turns, always surprising
Herself for the camera's eye: *Oh, who in the world*
Are you? And what on earth are you going to say?
An ice-blue damselfly swerves at her knee.

The sun goes dim. They wait with a casual boredom,
Indifferently regarding leaves and clouds
As matters of time. Then they see me
Sprawled in a shadow with an open notebook.

They take me in at a glance, calmly. I write
Some words to show I'm minding my own business.
They go on waiting for light
Like me, for a self-enchanting moment of April.

She smiles at some secret. She knows her audience
Of two is drinking her in, but remains faithful
To herself in her own fashion
As I must now, till the end of the session

When she rises (spiked heels shaky on spike moss)
To brush earthiness from her, stretches her arms,
And balances away through the yielding grass,
Not turning to look back.

The pond shimmers and clears. In its reflection
The shades of maple leaves recover the sky.

❧ *Photographing a Rattlesnake*

On smooth sand among stones
It stares more steadily
And lidlessly than the lens
Held near it, not hiding
Or posing, but simply there
In a dead calm, dead sure
Of the ways of its body
Around the maze past the end
Of nerves to the inmost
Rattle, but suddenly
The wedge of the blunt
Straightforward head, S-curve
Of muscle straight
Forward in a blur, mouth wide
For a down-slanted stabbing
Of fangs, a thump
At the camera's glassy eye,
Then a slow turning-away
Out of spirals from the sun
To shadows, to be scattered
Out of plain sight
Into mica spilled on pebbles
Over diamonds seen through
A teardrop of venom
Back to its still life.

❧ *An Address to Weyerhaeuser, the Tree-Growing Company*

After miles of stumps and slash and the once-buried endeavors
Of roots, all dozer-bladed to their logical ends, the clear-cut
Ends finally at a stand of firs near a creek, and for an hour
I've listened to what's left of the winter wrens
Claiming the little they can for territory.

(Which isn't much. And I'm too mad to be lyrical about it,
Lacking their grace, their fearlessness, their ingenuity.
Let somebody else do it: one of the most beautiful songs
In North America, a long, wild, ringing melody,
Says *The Complete Fieldguide to American Wildlife.* It lasts
For seven seconds with sixteen distinct notes and sixteen stops
Per second, an amazing 112 notes, says *Life Histories*
Of North American Birds. Our machines can barely track them.)

One comes to scout me where I sit on the last stump
Before the forest holds out its dark-green light again.
He sings, watching me. There's no use trying to say
What the music is like, cascading out of this short-tailed genius
Smaller than a mouse. Another answers and another,
Distinct though distant. I catch a glimpse of one through glasses
Down by the creek. Being as scientific as the next-to-last man,
I mark the spot and measure it off on the deep soft forest floor
(No rhapsodic passages about licorice fern and running pine and
    moss)
As clumsily as a moon-walker. His voice was carrying
Clearly and easily five hundred feet and could have reached
    further,
But I'll stay reasonably sober: this tiny groundling,
This incredibly gifted ounce was moving and reclaiming
A hemisphere of June air weighing nine tons.

Mr. Weyerhaeuser, your fallers and heavy thinkers made this
    possible.
I realize June is a distracting month: you must trap and kill
All those ravenous black bears whose berries haven't ripened

And who maul and gnaw a few of your billions of saplings
And you're looking forward to spraying the already dying
Tussock moths again, regardless of our expense, regardless
Of what else may be trying to live under the branches,
But for a moment consider *Troglodytes troglodytes,* this wren
Who has never forged a treaty or plotted a war
Or boasted of trying to serialize massacre after massacre
Or managed a forest or suffered the discomfort of an obituary
Listing credits in fraternal and charitable parlays
And other safe bets: he's moving a greater weight
Of living and dead matter daily than all your logging crews.
This creature smaller than your opposable thumb
And much more subtle is singing all day
In the woods you haven't clear-cut yet. Each song
Lasts seven seconds and forever. Think what you might manage
To move if you could sing or even listen.

✿ Staying Alive in a
Clear-cut Forest

I sit on a forest floor
That has lost its forest.
After five winters and Aprils
In the unaccustomed light
The groundlings have turned pale,
Wondering what and where
They are, having outlasted
One more dazzling summer:
Clubmoss and vine maple,
Bittercress, maidenhair,
Rush, sweet-after-death.

Around me, seedling firs,
Whose thick drought-toughened branches
Seem artfully dwarfed and maimed
By their masters like *bonsais*
Or like wind-shaped, sidewise
Godchildren of crownfires,
Are groping toward the sky
Again among rotten splinters
And the gray slabs of their elders
Slowly, outgrowing my anger
In the sawteeth of disaster.

To learn from the survivors
Skills I can only pray for,
I come back year after year
Like one of the outlanders
Growing beside me—clover,
Stonecrop, vetch, star thistle—
The perennial common strangers
Who thrive when the shade goes,
Who cast a few small shadows,
Who struggle in fading light,
Who will die in a green darkness.

❧ *The Shape*

The seed falls, lies still through rain,
Lies covered by snow through its after-ripening,
Then swells in the lengthening days
And bursts, and the primary root
Turns down to make its way
Through the newly dead and the long dead,
And the lateral roots spread wide
To brace for the lifting-up and the opening
Of the caul-pale embryo to the light,
And the roots deepen and darken, and the stem
Hardens and stiffens and lifts higher
The first unfolding leaves and the first branches,
And the roots embrace themselves, embrace stones,
Embrace the earth that holds them, sending their dream
High into the storms of the moon and wind,
The storms of the sun and stars for years.

What falls against the mind and lies still?—
Lies covered and cold, yet ripens,
Spreads down through a wealth of the half-remembered
And the forgotten, the unknown, to a deeper darkness,
To transparent eyes, to the ends of fingers, then raises
Into a storm this branched unreasoning shape?

❧ *Waterfall*

It plunges into itself, stone-white, mottled with emerald,
And finished falling forever, it goes on
Falling, half rain, to a pool
In bedrock and turns, extravagantly fallen, to recover
Its broken channel through maple and maidenhair
But always falling
Again, again, the same water, having been meanwhile
Everywhere under the moon, salted and frozen,
Thawed and upraised
Into its cloudy mother-of-pearl feathers to gather
Against the mountains, foregathering its own
And streaming once more
To fall as it must fall at the verge of understanding
In a roaring downpour as strange as this very moment
Swept over and over.

ꙮ *Trying to Sing in the Rain*

I sit by a steep deer-trail rapidly becoming
A small rapids with runoff from the rain
Higher in the woods, trying
To make one kind of song. The water falling around me
Has its own ideas about singing. It keeps running
Into my mouth and ears
And babbling better than I can, halfway up this mountain.
The runnel is flowing under me through a culvert
Into a stony creek that plunges
To a waterfall at a concourse of two creeks, and that stream
Falls to the river I see through a stand of cedars,
That river meeting another
River and together stretching wide to the ocean,
And I stretch wide more narrowly than the least
Members of this deep-green
Watershed, the swordfern, lichen, and moss beside me,
Yet all of us here take in more than we know,
Their cells and my soaking page
Gone blurred, but my heart at every heartbeat full and empty
By turns, as full and empty as the sky
By turns of the day and earth,
So recklessly happy I don't care if I'm out of kilter,
Far offkey, or taking an offbeat beating
And plummeling from my teacher,
The openhanded god of the storm who gives me this wrung-out
Singing and floating lesson, sending what passes
For my roots more rain
Than I can imagine how to use and washing my words
Away like part of the tumbling bedload
Of some wild river-to-be.

✤ *Three Ways of a River*

Sometimes, without a murmur, the river chooses
   The clearest channels, the easy ways
Downstream, dividing at islands equally, smoothly,
And meeting itself once more on the far side
   In a gathering of seamless eddies
That blend so well, no ripples rise to break

Into light like fingerlings taking their first mayflies
   Or, again, it will rush at overhangs
And blunder constantly against bare stone,
Against some huge implacable rock face
   To steepen and plunge, spring wide, go white,
And be dashed in tatters of spray, revolved and scattered

Like rain clouds pouring forward against a cliff
   In an endless storm of its own making,
While calmly a foot away lies the shape all water
Becomes if it flows aside into a pool,
   As still as the rock that holds it, as level
As if held cold to drink in these two hands.

❧ Making a Fire in the Rain

Rain has filled all these branches, living or broken,
And filled the river. I gather driftwood
And heap it on the stone-covered, shelving point
Where a man-sized backlog has beached itself,
And now the problem is obvious: nothing will burn
Willingly. Nothing wants to make fire but me.

Out of my half-remembered merit-badging,
I stack a pyramid of twigs and tinder,
Use myself as a lean-to, cheat with torn paper
And kitchen matches, and manage to start a flicker
That shifts, dodges, dies out, hisses, turns yellow,
Spits rain, reddens, then finally catches on.

I build it slowly toward branches thick as my arms
And cross them, smoking and steaming, over the heart.
I feed it and take Creator-Destroyer's pride
In this burning place, this point of consuming interest
Where my eyes follow each change of shape or color,
Direction or size, like an omen of pyromancy.

The backlog darkens: one hollow gives up the ghost
And shrinks to blackening cells, to cloistered charcoal.
It could have led dozens of other lives,
Been sawed or carved or pulped, stayed lost in the woods
To nurse new saplings and ferns, a bed for moss.
Instead, it starts a second death by fire.

Its leaves once hoarded the sun. That heat breaks out,
The river escapes it, sizzling, a stone explodes,
Rain slants, wind blusters among it, the flame huddles:
I share all these exchanges of elements,
Being pummeled by one and breathing still another
And sitting on the uncompromising third

And staring at the burnt crux of the fourth:
Fire and water and wind on this bare earth—
They know each other of old, even outside in,
But newcomers like me fumble among them
To search for Aqua Vitae, Philosopher's Stones,
The Inspiring Breath, the Refining Fire, Fool's Gold.

The rain is too much, suddenly, the wind deadly,
The stones too blunt, and the fire too close for comfort.
I get up no wiser, though now cured like a salmon,
And climb to the road, turning for one more look
At that obstinate tongue of light dwindling to nothing.
The smoke sweeps off downstream in a toppling column.

❧ *Driftwood*

From its burial at sea, a gray-white forest
Has come to Dungeness Spit to lie ashore:
Whole trees, their bark long-lost, their roots clutching
Only the wind, their jumbled branches
Smooth-sided schools of fish.

Not one of the thousands, thousands strewn for miles
Across and among each other, gnarled or straight
Or broken, level, slanted or half-buried
In sand, not one though dead and left
For dead gestures of storms,

For masters of seawrack done with dying now
In the salted calm of knots and rings and veins,
In every cell still held out to the light
Or the rain, having no more to do
With stretching and letting fall,

Not one though leafless, the green gone, cast away
And stranded here like the bones of forgotten seasons,
The bones of the dying gods of moving water
And weather, under our eyes or fingers
Not one not beautiful.

❧ *Snowflakes*

*Like most of the sky's snow, which
never comes to earth at all, even the
few flakes destined to reach the ground
linger interminably on their downward
journey—in some cases taking weeks
or months on the way . . .*
—Guy Murchie, *Song of the Sky*

They will not fall from high
Above earth, indifferently
Giving in by following
The impulses of others,
But move in their own ways
At a slant through wind after wind

To wobble eccentrically
Edgewise or spin or flutter
Like leaves or go steeply
Feathering down in swirls
Or spirals, each one falling
For days or whole seasons

From the moving peaks of clouds
Where, first by last, they honor
The clear six-crested law
Of their crystal lattices,
And now they are sailing
Softly to drifts at last,

But some, before touching, swerve,
Hover, and rise again,
Their old shapes changing
At first by dwindling, by losing
The small spread branches
They grew from seeds of dust,

Then stretching by gathering
The broken and the lost
Together, each like nothing
Ever before reborn
From the star-filled heart of water,
And stay in the sky forever.

〄 *There*

Where you haven't looked yet, there, in that passage
Between cattails, past the darker inlet,
Do you see it? You can't quite tell
What it is at first, and when you realize, finally,
How much of it is alive, it may seem the colors
Of death, an accident of commingled forms
And reflections, or there, beyond the reeds where the sky
Spills through the gray of a tattered season,
Do you see that shape on the shore as motionless
As the sand and the driftwood
At the rim of the dissolving mist? Or where the rush
Of the clear current has turned the light over stones
On the streambed to a wavering suppleness giving way
Like stems bent by a wind (but returning, returning)
Whose outlines are the water itself, do you see
There, if only for a moment, what you had almost
Forgotten you might still hope for?

Staying Found

We become lost not because of anything we do, but because of what we leave undone. . . . We stay found by knowing approximately where we are every moment. . . .
—Bradford Angier, *How to Stay Alive in the Woods*

He stood alone on the almost washed-away road
By the rain forest, caught by its impossible
Greenness. He started walking toward it, bewildered
By a wilderness he'd only half imagined
Among the mills and ruined lakes of his childhood.

He walked on moss as deep as his strange shoes
More softly than he'd ever walked, more quietly
In a rain that fell without falling, through an air
Softer than water, on earth, on a resurrected
Earth whose fire was wildflowers, glistening
Suns and moons of berries, dawns of gold lichen,
And scarlet sporophytes like spearheads guarding
A nurse-log where young cedars rose from the graves
Of ancestors, once two hundred or more feet
Above his feet and theirs, where huge others
Had closed a sky between him and the sky.

He stood among small perfectly neglected
And cared-for children in a virgin forest
And found himself. But when he turned, he was lost.

One moment he had been healed. He had forgotten
The defeated trees, the flowers starving
In poisonous wind and rain, the dead ground
Where he had tried to grow. In another moment,
He had learned a different way of dying
Called Here and Now, called There and Where and Nowhere.

When he stumbled onto the road again, his mind
Had changed. He was no longer lost in the woods
Or in cities as he had always been,
Not knowing it. Now, he would stay found.

Sequence:
Acts of
War

❧

❧ In Enemy Territory

There comes a time in going to war when the earth underfoot
Is yours no longer, when the country ahead
Is enemy territory,
Even green hillsides, orchards, and commonplace crossroads,
Unmanned stone walls by millstreams seeming at peace
With an inoffensive heaven,
And you, from that moment on, must assume sharp hostile eyes
Are aimed your way, wondering what you mean
On your line of advance
As you shift from point to point of natural cover.
As part of a greater movement, you understand
One bush at a time, one rock,
One stump, one ditch, one ruined house, revealing yourself
Suddenly, swiftly, then waiting motionless
For your human semblance
To disappear, to blend with your surroundings, to bring you
Through this struggle alive—no show of hands,
No rattling of steel,
No gestures or brave postures for the sake of monuments
Or memorials, no standing up to be counted,

No flagging of banners,
But only your straightforward face as you crouch and scuttle
And freeze again in some doubtful sanctuary,
In the shade of this tree
That chose its first last place to stand by the accidents
Of earth and rain, the trajectories of the seasons,
Where an overcast
Of bare branches has spread to intercept the bombardment
Of light that mottles and riddles your body
To innocent pieces.
You remember the land you left behind: you wandered there
All day or all night if you wished, at random,
Without hiding or trembling,
With no great need to think like an enemy or to see one
Falling in the distance, an anonymous blur,
Or to face one savagely
Hand to hand, or to meet one at all, let alone make him yours
In death and watch him signaling speechlessly
His utter surrender,
To see the whites of his eyes turn up like moons. That nightmare
Of the execution of love could end this war
Right where you are,
Not going on in a fight to the finish, but taking refuge
And laying down your arms where you might learn
(As a last full measure)
What your already fallen and transformed companions,
The flowers of generations, have been learning
To do without you
In a more perfect camouflage, a more perfect strategy
For the reengagement of a more perfect union
In your heart's conflict:
Going to ground again and quickening with the dead
To prove the gold green neutral fire of the sun
Is enough to live by.

Securing a House

You can't ignore that house.
If you pass it by, if you suppose
It's empty or pretend
You have nothing to fear from it
On your way to battle,
It may become a nest
For the enemy behind you,
So you pause now
And turn to the doorway.

What you're going to do
Is dangerously familiar:
You've crossed the thresholds
Of friends and strangers
Thousands of times, not standing
On ceremony, have taken the roofs
Of others over your head
For granted, feeling at ease,
Not wondering who might be hiding

From you, who might be lying
In wait at the dead end
Of a hallway, listening, thinking
Of you in the basement
Or the attic, not wanting you
To make yourself at home
But sketching plans for a future
That leaves you nothing at all
To look forward to.

Now slowly you prime yourself
For anything: four walls
At peace with their floors
And ceilings, emptiness, no one
In room after room

Or the wildest of faces
Rushing toward you, singing
And crying out loud
At the sight of a rescuer,

You, or a burst of fire
Out of nowhere, breaking
The heart of your position
Or from some innocent common
Object under your hand
An explosion
That throws you into a posture
Of defense, a *tableau mort*
In memoriam of your war.

≱ *To the Last Man*

At the point of farthest advance in the misfortunes
Of war, in the pitch and tossing-away of battle
When your sense of direction turns
Against you and it doesn't matter where
You align your sights or level your blank face
To know the enemy—that source of crossfire
And enfilading fire, that withering
Of overhead fragmentation and blazing flares,
That upheaval of landmines—when the chain of command
No longer connects you to superiors
But ends at its weakest link, you may find yourself
Alone at the break of morning, a one-man force
In a land whose landmarks blur your memories
Of maps and numbers, and all you see around you
Is wreckage and mud, the decay of comrades
At peace now in their newly disarmed divisions.

Yet if you seem to have nothing left worth doing
But joining that darker effort, that quieter chaos,
All may not be lost. For all you know,
You are the single unpredictable crucial
Element at a point of counterattack,
A voice come back from a body count of the dead
For a reckoning over bones that now depend
On you to make the most of what's left around them,
Not carcasses of the truth but the whole truth
Breathing and insane, of which you are the insane
Defender, your story as magically royally blooded,
As circled by fire, as holy, as otherworldly,
As dreadful as the world that dreamed it among
Ancestral voices prophesying you.
Even with no one listening, you must tell it.

❧ Victory

From the exhausted hoofbeats of the drums in the earth softly
At first to the bugles of engines coming the faint far-off
Screaming then bright at the parapet of your mouth your breath
Your fingers catching your opening eyes the whole blood
Rushing from heart to face to fulfill to overflow
Your stiffening body to leap your arms rising your hands
Held high you knew at last it was here it was all yours now.

❧ At Peace

After the splitting earth-
Work-battering nightmare
Of war that seemed
The downfall of the sky

Under fire, at the shock
Of morning, you've broken through
Beyond the battlefield
Into the open, where everything
You see—each hill, each pathway,
Each grove and wellspring
Under miraculously
Leaf-bearing, unshattered branches—
Is yours for the asking.

Here barbed wire means no end
To your life or your country
But a return to pasture
After pasture, where the flashing far off
And its following thunder
Are thunder and thunderbolt,
Not death, where the sound of trumpets
Overhead means no surrender
Or dawn raid or burial
But your small share of glory:
The cry of the wild geese.
From houses ahead, the children
Are already running and shouting
Toward you, unafraid,
And the faces all turned to you
At windows see no hero,
No star-born conquerer,
But you, their living message,
Speechless and empty-handed.

Four

❧ After Reading Too Many Poems, I Watch a Robin Taking a Bath

For James Wright

She does it so devotedly
In the middle of her most ecstatic spasm
There seems to be no water
In the murky birdbath at all.

It's all in the air
At once, all showering above
Her paddling wings or running
Among her feathers spread like fingers.

She crouches, puffs the white down
Of her underbreast as if settling
On something pale blue, and the water gathers
Beneath her, against her.

Now she thinks a long moment
Without thinking, stares
North and south at the same time
At nothing.

And suddenly she's all done with it,
Up on the dripping edge, shaking
And sleek, alert, herself again,
Flying into hiding.

❧ Applying for a Loan with the Help of the Dictionary of Occupational Titles

You're a what?
—Question from a Credit Manager

In my other lives, I've been a sheepskin pickler,
A bowling-ball engraver, a feather washer,
Banana dispatcher, and wild cherry dipper.
I've been a bologna lacer and beeswax bleacher.
I've balanced fans, dried germs, and dipped balloons,
Served as a bellyman and a skull grinder
And saved my bacon once as a butt presser.

I've tackled even more mysterious Labors:
I've been a burning foreman, an apron scratcher,
Bar creaser, chill man, backside polisher,
Flyaway clerk, head chiseler, lingo cleaner,
Crotch joiner, hardness tester, and beat-out boy,
So don't go thinking, because I say I'm a poet,
Sir, I don't know serious work pays off.

Ode to the Muse on Behalf of a Young Poet

Madam, he thinks you've become his lover. He doesn't know
        You're his landlady,
The keeper of the keys to the front door, the mistress
Of the stairwell, postmistress, indifferent cook, shade-lifter
Veiled by twitching curtains, protectress of thermostats,
        Handmaiden of dust.

He doesn't see your crowsfeet or cracked smile or the grayness
        Swept from your temples.
To him, your odor of mothballs is the heady essence
Of the Gardens of Inspiration and your bed-ridden houseplants
The Garden itself. Look, he has begun to scribble.
        Grant him your mercy.

If you should tell him he's behind in his rent instead,
        You may startle him
Out of a year's growth of beard and spirit. Consider
Your reputation, not as a bill collector, but as the sole
Distributor of Sparks, Flashes, and Sudden Leaps
        From the Visionary Aether.

His heart's in the right place: in his mouth. If he means
        Anything, he means well.
If he means nothing to you, why not amuse him for a brief
Lifetime with the benefit of your doubt? What would you be
Without him and his attentions but an empty housekeeper,
        A closet hostess?

Who else could be more ardent, more flattering? Already
        He's wondering where you are.
He's inventing enough implausible, brilliant rivals to last you
Forever. He wouldn't dream of asking you to wash
His unmentionable linen or scrub his floor or thaw his dinner.
        He's starving for you.

Blank paper pays you no honor. Using your name in vain
                    Is his only blasphemy.
Go to him now in disguise and comfort him with all
Your charm-filled anger, your dreadful, withering beauty,
Your explosive silences, the consolations of horror,
                    The forgeries of death.

❧ *Book Sale—Five Cents Each!*

On the Salvation Army's bookshelves, the derelicts
Line up as if for coffee,
Some stuck together like doughnuts, some mumbling music
To warm up charity:
The soaked hymnals, the self-devotional memoirs
Droning Vanity, Vanity,
The loud reports from the Corporals of Industry
Now muffled by mildew,
The Rover Boys strung far Out West, blind-canyoned
By a ripped-off chapter,
And the backs of the books-of-the-month-after-month
Humped undercover,
The indigestible digests, the spiral schoolbooks
Telling and telling
What they're going to tell, then telling, now telling no one
What they told each other—
Rank after rank gone by the reviewing stand
To join this cold Army,
For hire, five cents forever, cheaper than kindling
If it comes to burning.
But *Laugh with Leacock* and *Laughing Boy* and *Memento Mori,*
All Quiet on the Western Front,
Come as you are, with dust on your riddled jackets,
Though your wounds need binding,
Oh, *Adam and Eve and Pinch Me, Beau Geste,* and *Victory,*
Come home to dinner.

❧ On Motel Walls

Beyond the foot of the bed: a seascape whose ocean,
Under the pummeling of a moon the shape and shade
Of a wrecking ball, is breaking into slabs
Against a concrete coast. Next to the closet:
A landscape of pasty mountains no one could climb
Or fall from, beyond whose sugary grandeur
Lies Flatland, a blankness plastered on plasterboard.
And over the bed: a garden in the glare
Of shadowless noon where flowerheads burst more briefly
And emptily and finally than fireworks.

For hours, I've been a castaway on that shore
By that fake water where nothing was ever born,
Where the goddess of beauty sank. I've flopped on those slopes
Where no one on earth could catch a breath worth breathing,
And I've been caught in that garden
Where the light is neither waves nor particles
But an inorganic splatter without a source.

Tonight, what's in the eye of this beholder
Is less and less and all the ways I can go
Dead wrong myself through the quick passing
Of sentences: tomorrow, I may be staring
Straight in the face of the hanging judge of my future
Who'll read me with the deadpan of a jailer
Before a search, a lock-down, and lights out.
I'll do hard time all night inside these walls
In my mind's eye, a transient facing a door
That says, *Have you forgotten anything
Of value? Have you left anything behind?*

❧ Neighbors

My neighbor tells me I'm the worst, the rudest
Person he's ever met. He's waved. His wife
Has waved at me. They've said *Hello*
There from their own yard through waving branches
Squarely over the fence my way. His face
Whose name I hurriedly remember is furious
Across our year-old border at not being
Waved at, livid, pinching itself shut.

I tell him no that can't be me, it isn't
Like me at all to be snobbish, to dream up grudges
Like a neighbor's keeper: sometimes I have problems
With focusing tunnel vision, my outer ears
Have hard-of-hearing sinuses—or words
To that tongue-tied effect. I'm afraid to tell him
I'm trying hard to listen to other voices
In my private head, not necessarily
Including his, to say I'm too wrapped up
In my own thoughts for fear he'll challenge me
To name one. I can't tell him I see things
Like trees instead of his face, that I hear birds
Instead of his wife because I imagine
Myself belonging among those stranger neighbors.

His eyes come open narrowly. His mouth
Returns in a manner of speaking
Reluctantly: well, maybe he misjudged me,
Turning away to mull me over. Later
That evening he and his wife ride slowly by
On bikes, maneuvering close to where I've wandered
To be with a young maple, waving, crying
Out loud *Hello there,* making their good feelings
Perfectly clear at last to the handicapped.

❧ *Poem About Breath*

(a memory of Elizabeth Bishop, 1950)

She was at work on a poem about breath.
She asked what punctuation might be strongest
For catching her breath, for breath catching
Halfway in her throat, between her straining breastbone
And her tongue, the bubbly catching of asthma.

She didn't care for ellipses or blank spaces.
Would a double colon work? Or Dickinson dashes?
It wouldn't be right for breath to have full stops.
It *does* go on, though people with trouble breathing
Think about it, and breathe, and think about it.

They think too many times of clearing the air
They have to breathe, about the air already
Down there in their lungs, not going out
On time, in time, and when it's finally gone,
Not coming back to the place longing to keep it.

Each breath turns into a problem like a breath
In a poem that won't quite fit, giving the wrong
Emphasis to a feeling or breaking the rhythm
In a clumsy way, where something much more moving
Could happen to keep that poem moving and breathing.

She said as a child she'd learned *one* different style
Of breathing, and her eyelids lowered and darkened.
She bowed her full, firm, pale, remarkable face,
Then solemnly lifted it and opened her mouth,
Stuck out her curled-back tongue and, while it quivered,

Unfolded it slowly, balancing near the end
A half-inch bubble of saliva, gleaming.
With her lightest breath, she puffed it, and it floated

Through late-summer light along the workroom window
All the way to the sill before it broke.

Then she bent over and over, choking with laughter.

ꙮ Catching the Big One
at Lone Lake

A memory of Richard Hugo, 1956

From the rowboat, loosely tied
To a broken dock, he glared
At the enemy in the distance:
The other fishermen catching
The brightest living silver
For themselves. For him, nothing.

He'd expected nothing, he said,
As usual. What else was new?
It was just like writing poems:
Dumb luck sometimes. He glanced
Up shore to a weedy house
Where nothing was waiting.

And then he hooked the lunker.
As he rose to his bare feet
In its honor, it rose too,
Wildly, an outsized rainbow
In rainbows, whose highest leap
Sent it whirligigging sideways

To the dock where it fishtailed
Head first down through a hole
In the planks to splash once more
Out of sight. And almost sinking
Both of us, ankle deep
Among empties and sandwiches,

Deep-sixing his rod and reel,
He went after it, scrambled and slammed
Down in a belly-flop
Across loose rotten boards,
Guided the taut line clear
Of snags, then hand over hand,

Slowly, against each change
Of direction, each quick lunge,
Brought up into the light
(As gaping and round-eyed
And astonished as *he* was) the one
That didn't get away.

❧ Eulogy for Richard Hugo
(1923–1982)

We both wore masks. Mine over my mouth
Was there to catch each word, each dangerous breath
Before it reached the man sitting in bed
And found its way through his defenseless blood.
His mask was a royal bruise across his chest
(Where one lung labored, labored hard as Christ
To cure the marrow that had turned against him)
And the swollen flesh of a face, once lean and handsome,
Now stretched past guilt and fear, past innocence
And courage into a skin-tight radiance.

While blood hung on a scaffold, dripping warm
And slow to its cold future in his arm,
He talked of jobs and money and old games,
Of letters and love, good humor and bad dreams,
Of what he'd learned, in pain, about his lives,
Of struggles between his better and bitter halves.

For thirty years I'd known a starving child
Inside him, tough and subtle, shrewd and squalid,
Who shared his body, glaring through his eyes
And balking at the cost of wretchedness.
Outside, he wore a life intensely human
And over that, at times, like a mad shaman,
The skulls of enemies and the skins of beasts,
Tatters of beggar boys and family ghosts—
Sacred disguises. "What I do is me"
Became for him "What I seem, we all may be."

These struggling selves made poems, did without
The gibberish of God, grudge-matching wit,
The urge to pose or maunder, prattle or preach,
And sang blunt beautiful American speech
In voices none of us had heard before,
Whose burden was "We can grow up through fear."

He spent his days in search of a hometown
Where he could be class hero and class clown,
Unknown and famous, friendly and alone:
Wearing his old school colors, the gray and white
Of ashes, he lies there now, its laureate.

Elegy While Pruning Roses

What saint strained so much,
Rose on such lopped limbs to a new life?
—Theodore Roethke

I've weeded their beds, put down manure and bark dust.
Now comes the hard part: theoretically
It has to be done, or they spend their blooming season
In a tangle of flowerless, overambitious arms.
So here go pruning shears in spite of the thorns
That kept off browsers for all the millennia
Before some proto-dreamer decided roses
Were beautiful or smelled their unlikely promise.

Reluctantly I follow the book and stunt them
In the prescribed shapes, but throwing cuttings away
Over the fence to die isn't easy.
They hang onto my gloves and won't let go,
Clutching and backlashing as if fighting
To stay in the garden, but I don't have time or patience
To root them in sand, transplant them, and no room
In an overcrowded plot, even supposing
They could stand my lame midhusbandry.
So into limbo with all these potential saints.

Already the ladybugs, their black-dotted orange
Houses always on fire, are climbing for aphids,
And here come leaf-rollers, thrips and mildew
To have their ways. I've given up poison:
These flowers are on their own for the spring and summer.
But watching the blood-red shoots fade into green
And buds burst to an embarrassing perfection,
I'll cut bouquets of them and remember
The dying branches tumbling downhill together.

Ted, you told me once there were days and days
When you *had* to garden, to get your hands

Down into literal dirt and bury them
Like roots to remind yourself what you might do
Or be next time, with luck. I've searched for that mindless
Ripeness and found it. Later, some of these flowers
Will go to the bedside of the woman I love.
The rest are for you, who weren't cut off in your prime
But near the end of a long good growing season
Before your first frost-bitten buds.
You knew where roots belonged, what mysterious roses
Come from and were meant for: thanks,
Apology, praise, celebration, wonder,
And love, in memory of the flourishing dead.

❧ *Part Song*

At the nursing home's Thanksgiving party
The janitor is singing "Trees"
Better than anyone could have hoped for.
All of us, old and older, are shedding leaves.

He sings in a heart-failed baritone
As if he meant each lame, unlikely word,
And all of us are changing color
Over tea and cookies and clumsy conversation.

As if I'd meant each lame, blind, halting word
Long ago, I'm choking over my lost mother
Over coffee and cake and vacant conversations.
She used to sing it better than I expected.

And here I'm choking over my grandmother
And my wife beside her and all the missing singers.
We used to live as well as we could hope for.
We used to sing in the morning like young robins.

My wife beside herself and the missing singers
Applaud when "Trees" is over, whispering thank you.
We used to sing in our cages like starved robins.
Now we sit still, not looking at God all day.

When the applause dies down, we're mumbling thank you,
Thank you for singing anything, even that.
Now some sit still as God, making no trees.
All their gray mouths lie open as if singing.

God, thank them for singing anything, even nothing.
The snow on their bosoms drifts a little further.
All their gray mouths lie open for more snow.
The earth's sweet breast is flowing away from them.

❧ Into the Nameless Places

Mr(s) ——— *is undergoing Reality Orientation to help him/her remember who and where he/she is. Please include the following questions in your conversation with him/her.*
—notice on a nursing home wall

Your name is?

      Not on the tip of my tongue, but slipping away
      And only half-returning when I call it
      To mind, to mind me like a child
      As it used to when I recited it
      More clearly and easily than any other answer.
      It waits shyly, a little way off, uncertain
      Whether it must come back to touch my lips
      Or whether I'll follow it slowly in good time
      Into the nameless places it longs for.

The date is?

      All of the hundred, all of the twelve,
      All of the thirty, the seven, the twenty-four,
      All of the sixty, all of the sixty.

The weather is?

      On the other side of the window where it waits
      Or wanders, either a blurred brightness
      Or a blurred gray through which everything rises
      That wants to rise, then gathers to rise
      Again, out of reach, beyond me, without me.

Tomorrow is?

      As it may be or as it was
      Yesterday, and ever shall be in the beginning
      Of sleep and the end of waking, both meeting
      Like upper and lower eyelids, as silently
      As eyelids rising and falling, lashes touching
      In the calm storm of the darkness.

Your birthday is?

      This morning again, and again the years
      Repeating themselves as fervently as wishes,

The many happy returns of wax and smoke
Like my breath passing away over the face
Of sweetness, layer by layer, crumbling, breathless.
You were born in the city of?
In the walled city of a hospital among nurses
And hands and sheets where all the furniture
Rolls slowly away over the bare floors,
And my sainted aunts surround me
With murmurous attention, all but one:
The dark lady-in-waiting whose needle
Sews up the doors and windows, gives this castle
The long rest of its life, its retiring beauty,
And no one asks me what the music means
Coming from the walls, the music ending
Only when the lights go dim. It sings
In place of my voice, keeping time and never
In need of any reminder to be over
In order to make room for the next beginning,
And no one asks if I wish to be
Anyone else or called anyone younger
Or where these rootless flowers have come from,
What gardens must still be growing somewhere
To pour such color against colorless pillows
Or why everyone is too far away
To kiss me, so lost beside me,
Even inside my arms, and no one
Asks out of politeness why I stare at nothing
As if it were really here.

❧ *The Death of the Moon*

Through the long death of the moon, we drank her light
As slowly as snow-melt, bearing her funeral
Against the turn of the earth by nights like flares
As she fell westward, trailing a torn shroud
Across the mountains, over the ashen water.

Our feet washed pale as shell, we faltered
After her, naming all she could answer,
But she turned her cold, lopsided face
Further away than we could follow.

She shrank to half a skull,
Sinking as if to sleep
At the salt edge of her grave.

Then her white knife,
Her closing eyelid.

Her darkness.

❧ The Astronomer's Apprentice

Some dark shadows were soon noticed crossing the
Sun, and afterwards some light streaks . . . their
frequency first and then their uniformity of
direction . . . indicating that an unusual
phenomenon was in progress. . . ."
—summary of a letter from Mysore Province, India, *Royal*
Astronomical Society, Monthly Notices, 1870

Observing the noon sun over Bangalore
Through a five-inch equatorial refractor,
Professor A. S. Herschel's assistant saw
Odd shadows move across that circle of fire
And beyond its borders where, against the sky
Like streams of meteors, they turned luminous.

Rubbing his eyes, he ruled out sparks and birds,
Then made his notes: *Motion irregular*
Like particles suspended in cross currents;
Their number anything short of infinite;
Distance uncertain; spectrum solar; brightness
Diminishing as they leave the edge of the disc;

Their form like halfmoons sailing diameter
Forward or edgeways; sometimes almost stellar,
Distinct and brilliant; at others, double crescents
Crossbarred, trailing winglike appendages.
In Professor Herschel's absence, he beamed with joy
And traced these mysteries to the brim of evening.

He saw his fortune there in a gold shower
Bearing his name with other great dead lucky
Stargazers who had brought new wonders to light,
Who'd fixed their positions with cartographers
And now lay scattered along the bright ecliptic
Like gods and heroes drawn into constellations.

That night he even dreamed the envious demons
That ruled the world were driven by Lord Vishnu
(The All-pervader on his giant bird)
To dance a lament on fire across the heavens
Forever, and he alone, like a favorite prince
Among earthlings, had been chosen as a witness.

All the next day he marked time with his fame
And tracked the procession north into a dazzling
Pavilion raised for a Lord of Astronomers.
On the third day, there fell at Hyderabad
Three hundred miles to the north a cloud of locusts
That ravaged everything green under the sun.

❧ *Medusa's Lover*

Her personal problems seemed unbearably
Embarrassing to Medusa: she hadn't a thing
To wear in public, and classical drapery
Did nothing to hide the hard-core facts of her figure,
And even the warmest, frilliest underclothes
Left her underworld colder. Her dreadful sisters,
Instead of comforting her in her misery,
Proved being a Gorgon ran in the family,
And she couldn't do a thing with her snaky hair
But feed it eggs and mice so it wouldn't, at night,
Hiss her awake or slither into her ears,
And worst of all, men couldn't catch her eye
Without turning as stony-faced as statues.

But suddenly one day to her amazement
She saw a young man shuffling toward her sideways,
Holding a shield like a mirror. He was staring
At her reflection, and though he wasn't too gorgeous
Himself—shoes down at the winged heels
And matted with mud, his roomy helmet wobbling
Around his head, the hem of his cloak sagging—
He was vastly more appealing than mere high-fliers,
Invincible soldiers, or invisible heroes:
He was looking at her and wasn't petrified.

She opened her arms to him. She lurched to meet him.
Her hair was hissing (in chorus) a wild love song.
She saw the gift he'd brought her: a gleaming, slender,
Adamantine sickle to wear like a queen's pendant
At her throat forever. She lifted her chin. She pursed.
She closed her eyes to wait for her first kiss.

❧ Pandora's Dream

Falling asleep, she saw the lid of the box
Beside her glittering, the unknown dowry
She was forbidden to look at,
But under eyelids heavier than moonlight
She carried that glitter down into a dream.

She was in the dark, in a chamber, touching its walls
And floor and ceiling with pieces of herself,
Some glinting like fireflies, some burnt black and cold,
Odd flapping and squirming pieces, feathered
And furred, bone-pointed, clawed, all wanting out.

But there was nowhere to go, no door, no window.
She was trapped as if in a box. Then with a groan
Of hinges, the ceiling opened,
And there in the widening strip of light, grown huge
And terrible, her own face looked in.

And all those parts of her in a swarm went flying
Upward and outward: maggots with bat wings,
Pink termites, scarlet bees, green wasps in a fury
And moths on fire like twistings of paper
And through them a death-squeaking of black mice.

She became that other holding the lid upraised
And wishing what she'd scattered would return
And shut itself in again to be forgotten,
That the god who'd cursed her with this gift
Would relent and rescue her from a curious heart.

She woke, she stretched, she forgot, she yawned, she saw
Only a box at her bedside, shimmering
With promises she could keep or break by lifting
A single clasp and using her naked eyes.
She rose, still in a dream, and opened it.

✤ *Sleeping Beauty*

The hard part wasn't the overgrown, thorn-clawed hedge
Between the Prince and what was supposed to be
A Beauty destined for him: rose vines gave way
Like an admiring crowd at an execution.

It wasn't the sight of the horses, hounds, and pigeons
Dozing, covered with leaves, in the courtyard,
Or the kitchen fire stopped cold under the spit
Or the flies on the wall, still in a dream-molasses.

And it wasn't the tableau of the maid plucking
A hundred-year-old chicken, or the cook
Caught in the act of tweaking the scullery boy.
He got through those and the cobwebs strung among them

Serene as an heir apparent inspecting corpses.
It wasn't even the King and Queen out cold
On their thrones: the finest dust had smoothed their cheeks,
Had padded the floor, wiped out the tapestries,

And drifted against the unusually polite,
Unnaturally silent ladies-in-waiting
(Prone and supine) and knights as limp as their garters.
But nothing kept him from the winding staircase.

And it wasn't the sight of Sleeping Beauty either.
All her sweet face, though grimy, was meant for kissing.
He puckered, rehearsed in midair, and it seemed easy.
Not even touching cold lips was the hard part.

He touched them. He stood still. He hoped for the best.
(She was the best. Everyone said so.
She was modest and honey-natured, a surefire handful.)
But Sleeping Beauty sat up like Waking Ugly.

She opened one red eye on the Good World,
Bored with it instantly. She had been certain
It had disappeared forever. But here it was: morning,
And time to get up again to be good for nothing.

It had been *exactly* like that from the beginning:
She was too good to be true, a basket case
In a doll basket, pink and gold, as dainty
As a rich dessert with whipped cream and meringue

To be nibbled between meals with smacks of the tongue
And kitchy-coos. But she grew up too true
To be good. Though no one coaxed her to be bad,
Slowly she figured it out, all by herself.

When was life going to happen? Honest to goodness,
Wasn't she honest as the day was long?
But it was *long*. Goodness seemed even longer
Through those long days and evenings till she could dream.

*Day*dreaming didn't do it. She could imagine,
Sure, being humped and crotchety like a witch
Or slick-lipped and languorous like a courtside doxy,
Or cockeyed, creepy, a minimum-lethal-dose

Of a daughter, a whiny changeling whose gold pillow
Belonged *under* the bed where bitches chewed gristle.
But something would always break into those daydreams—
A chuckle under the chin by a cockalorum,

A pinch in the box reserved for royal parties,
Or some Great Oaf like *this* at her bedside.
While she rolled over, snuggling herself to sleep,
He came to the hard part: Getting Out of There.

He scrambled down the steps, dodged broken-field
Through the throne room where a mixed gaggle of churls
And their grubby, groggy derelict Highnesses
Reared up in rags, all gaping at each other,

Ran past the maid and boy now plucking the cook,
Past flies studding the spitted ham like cloves
Over a fire gone out (with a puff of relief),
Past naked pigeons on clumps of molted feathers,

Past hounds heel-nipping the horses like hyenas,
And into the gloomiest, thickest part of the thicket
Where a hundred skeletons of his predecessors
(Each, once upon a time, Prince of the Year)

Leaned among brambles, wringing their knucklebones
To welcome him, grinning, covered with roses.

❧ Prince Charming

No matter what he did, his entourage said
How charming, wasn't that charming, did you hear
And see what he said and did, he couldn't be
Anything in the world but a Prince Charming.

When he polkaed, his mistakes were the variations
Taught by all dancing masters. If he revealed
The wrong socks wrong side out, they were the rage,
The unchangeable fashion-craze, till he could change them.

When he strolled nearby, young women were all eyes,
All ears, all thumbs, all Orange Maids delighted
To lead him on through secret passageways
To the Theater of Love and their seats of passion.

If he hunted or caroused, the brightest young men
Turned out for the party and uncorked his flagons.
If he raised a lance, a thousand and one knights
Buzzed at his plumes and bumbled around his armor.

But when it was curtains at the play, those women
(Like the entrances and exits and sound effects)
Seemed overly familiar, the acting acting.
On the hunt, the chase, or under the groaning board,

Instead of bawdy cronies and champions
Raising sweet hell on the Field of the Cloth of Gold,
He had tuft-hunters and saddle-hogs and bores
And gamy smell-feasts stuffing their breastplates.

No foe attacked him. His army horsed around
And around the castle, playing at swordplay
Till the dinner gong. He had a Chamber of Horrors
Yet no one used it but the Chamber of Commerce.

If he went questing, brambles lined up their thorns
And raked his byways. Sleet in the winter wind
Skidded to a halt. The sun in the summer doldrums,
While others swore and sweltered, fanned him balmy.

Instead of roaring for blood, monsters and giants
Shuffled and grinned at him, and damsels on rocks
With nothing to wear but chains from prior engagements
Suddenly found themselves free for the evening.

All his charmed life, nothing had gone wrong:
No witch at his cradle, no uncles foul as their plots,
No father substitutes with poisoned bonbons,
No spells to send him chasing wild mother geese.

His court was having a ball, but the Prince wasn't.
One night he'd had enough: he belched in their faces.
He slouched and picked his ears. He scratched his armpits
And, sucking his teeth, yawned till his jaw cracked.

Before they could say how charming it all was
And peck and cluck and crow the New Etiquette
From pillar to bedpost, up the barberpole,
And out to the last dunghill, he dismissed them.

He discharged his privy jesters and bathmates
And cushion-fluffers, the lapdogs at each thigh,
The footmen at each foot and the underfootmen,
Then flopped on his bed without a charm to his name.

He tossed and moaned. He bawled at the empty chamber:
"The stableboy was horsewhipped by a centaur!
The bailiff was disorganized by a warlock
And fed to a cockatrice! The arrowsmith

"Was stuck in the bull's-eye by a unicorn!
They lived full lives, but nothing happens to *me!*"
A pouf of sequins, a shimmer of shot silk,
And his Fairy Godfather popped out of the closet.

"You get three choices: one—an overgrown palace.
Hundreds of sleepers, including bugs on the wall
And a princess cute as a bug. You're in. You kiss her.
She and the crowd wake up, and you get married.

"Two—a girl in the woods in a glass casket.
Seven old runts for sextons and altar boys.
Songbirds carrying daisies. She's dead but cute.
You kiss her. She blinks. She coughs up an apple core.

"Her stepmother has a fit, and you get married.
Or three—at a dance, you fall for a flashy teaser.
She runs away but tosses a glass slipper
With her number in it. You trace her rats and pumpkins.

"And she's there! With grating sisters! A cindery mother!
But the shoe has the fit this time, and you get married.
Now take your choice." "Which one makes me a hero?
Do I ever grow up? Do I ever get to be old?"

"You get to be Prince Charming." "But isn't there something
A little more unfortunate and romantic?"
"Don't call me, I won't call you." His godfather vanished,
And the Prince sprawled on his bed like a total loss.

But through his casement he heard a lovely croaking
As squalid as bog mold. It called him, and spiraling
Downstairs with a hop, a skip, and a silent slither,
He slipped through the door and out into the night.

It came from the wishing well, but his knees and feet
Went gawky and slipshod, his fingers melted together,
So he squatted forward scrunchbacked on all fours
And plumped along more easily on his belly.

The sounds grew louder. There on the mossy well-curb,
Making galumphs, cabooming, cricketing high
And low, promising havens of mudbaths
And heavens of squishiness, a green girl waited.

He felt his eyes grow huge and his mouth broaden.
He felt his skin flush green and break out in stripes
At the sight of her. Though his tongue was a springy mouthful,
He did his best and croaked, "What happens now?"

"We do whatever jumps out of our heads
And make our own story." With a glorious leap
She sailed into the well. He tumbled after,
And they sang offkey and on till it was morning,

Till it was evening and dawn again, and morning
After morning, they sang one story after another
Out of their heads—lost tales of pollywogs—
And charmed that kingdom with their slapdash chorus.

✿ The Author Says Goodbye to His Hero

It always seemed obvious what you had to do
Back there at the beginning of the story:
Survive by hacking your way
Past giants and ogresses and clumsy monsters
And witches in the woods toward your true calling
Come lightning, come darkness.
Compared to you, those minor characters
With all their ambushes and bellowing
Seemed incidental tricks,
The harmless, happy accidents due your rank,
Suspenseful nicks in the sword-edges of time.
You left them all
Behind you, forgotten. You were the only one
Going somewhere important, whose life was a wonder
Among wonders, both charmed
And charming against the dullness of those others
Left swollen or headless by the side of the road.
But now, without a chance
To suit yourself to new armor, without warning,
No magic in your words, no light-fingered gifts
Picked up from sorcerers,
And no more suddenly gorgeous messages
Whispered into your ear by gods or demons,
You're on your own.
We're parting company. From this page on,
It's another story, and you won't know quite how
Seriously it may take you:
The very next page you turn may turn out to be
Blank or, worse, may go on twisting and turning
Without your name.
You may even see in a clearing someone striding
Toward you like yourself in a cracked mirror,
A furious fellow-hero
Blundering past your guard and passing behind you.
If so, you may have lost what you thought you'd mastered.
He's on a quest to outdo

All your moon-stricken ventures, his sword even more
Relentlessly carving a trail like the trailblazing
Of blood-red watchfires,
And ahead of you: his abandoned castle, the drawbridge
Down, the feast laid out, brave music,
The throne empty,
And strangers braced for your story's end. No man
Can tell you which will be yours then: princess or crown
Or the glint of the ax.

❧ *Lament for the Nonswimmers*

They never feel they can be well in the water,
Can come to rest, that their bodies are light.
When they reach out, their cupped hands hesitate:
What they wanted runs between their fingers.
Their fluttering, scissoring legs sink under.

Their bones believe in heaviness, their ears
Shake out the cold invasion of privacy,
Their eyes squeeze shut. Each breath,
Only half air, is too breathtaking.
The dead man's float seems strictly for dead men.

They stand in the shallows, their knees touching,
Their feet where they belong in the sand.
They wade as carefully as herons, but hope for nothing
Under the surface, that wilderness
Where eels and sharks slip out of their element.

Those who tread water and call see their blurred eyes
Turn distant, not away from a sky's reflection
As easy to cross as the dependable earth
But from a sight as blue as drowned men's faces.
They splash ashore, pretending to feel buoyant.

✿ *The Naval Trainees Learn How to Jump Overboard*

The last trainees are climbing the diving tower
As slowly as they dare, their fingers trembling
On the wet rungs, bare feet reluctantly
Going one step higher, one more, too far
Above the water waiting to take them in.

They stand on top, knees slightly buckled, nowhere
To put their hands, all suddenly thinking how
Good it's always been to be braced up
By something, anything, but ready to be let down
By their loud instructor thirty feet below.

They are the last ones learning how to jump
Feet-first into the swimming pool, to windward
From an imagined ship (in case of drift or fire),
Their ankles crossed, their loose life jackets held
Down with one hand, their noses pinched with the other.

They pause at the edge. Only one second away
From their unsupported arches, the surface glitters,
Looking too solid, too jagged and broken,
A place strictly for sinking, no place to go.
Each has his last split-second second thoughts.

Others are treading water, hooting and whistling
Abandon Ship and General Alarm,
But these stare toward the emptiest of horizons.
Upright, blue-lipped, no longer breathing, already
Drowned, they commit their bodies to the deep.

✣ *In Distress*

(Selected entirely from International Code of Signals, *United States Edition, published by U.S. Naval Oceanographic Office)*

I am abandoning my vessel
Which has suffered a nuclear accident
And is a possible source of radiation danger.
> *You should abandon your vessel as quickly as possible.*
> *Your vessel will have to be abandoned.*

I shall abandon my vessel
Unless you will remain by me,
Ready to assist.
I have had a serious nuclear accident
And you should approach with caution.
The position of the accident is marked by flame.
The position of the accident is marked by wreckage.
I need a doctor. I have severe burns.
I need a doctor. I have radiation casualties.
I require a helicopter urgently, with a doctor.
The number of injured or dead is not yet known.
Your aircraft should endeavor to alight
Where a flag is waved or a light is shown.
Shall I train my searchlight nearly vertical
On a cloud intermittently and, if I see your aircraft,
Deflect the beam upwind and on the water
To facilitate your landing?
> *I do not see any light.*

You may alight on my deck; I am ready to receive you forward.
You may alight on my deck; I am ready to receive you amidship.
You may alight on my deck; I am ready to receive you aft.
> *I am entering a zone of restricted visibility.*
> *Visibility is decreasing.*
> *You should come within visual signal distance.*

I require immediate assistance; I have a dangerous list.
I require immediate assistance; I have damaged steering gear.
I require immediate assistance; I have a serious disturbance on
    board.

I require immediate assistance; I am on fire.

> *What assistance do you require?*
> *Can you proceed without assistance?*
> *Boats cannot be used because of weather conditions.*
> *Boats cannot be used on the starboard side because of list.*
> *Boats cannot be used on the port side because ot list.*
> *Boats cannot be used to disembark people.*
> *Boats cannot be used to get alongside.*
> *Boats cannot be used to reach you.*
> *I cannot send a boat.*

I require immediate assistance; I am drifting.

I am breaking adrift. I have broken adrift.

I am sinking.

> *Did you see the vessel sink?*
> *Is it confirmed that the vessel has sunk?*
> *What is the depth of water where the vessel sank?*
> *Where did the vessel sink?*
> *I have lost sight of you.*

My position is doubtful.

My position is ascertained by dead reckoning.

Will you give me my position?

> *You should indicate your position by searchlight.*
> *You should indicate your position by smoke signal.*
> *You should indicate your position by rockets or flares.*

My position is marked by flame.

My position is marked by wreckage.

Are you in the search area?

> *I am in the search area.*

Are you continuing to search?

> *Do you want me to continue to search?*
> *I cannot continue to search.*

I cannot save my vessel.

Keep as close as possible.

I wish some persons taken off.

A skeleton crew will remain on board.

You should give immediate assistance to pick up survivors.

You should try to obtain from survivors all possible information.
I cannot take off persons.
There are indications of an intense depression forming.
The wind is expected to veer.
You should take appropriate precautions.
A phenomenal wave is expected.
I cannot proceed to the rescue.
I will keep close to you during the night.
Nothing can be done until daylight.

🌿 *Stiltwalker*

Look up out tilting through
Into the light see higher
Than elephant howdahs the man
Who's all dressed up to go
Somewhere ahead to a tall
Mad party of one as the red
White blue tophatter wham
Flash bam from the oh say Uncle
Sam crash thank you how do
You like the weather up there
Too far in the first place
To stand step-laddering huge
At a time the only way
To go crookedly straight
Forward three-ringing around
Sawdusty spotlights never
Stopping so far from something
Upright to lean on handy
Goodbye already waving
Hello as soon as he's where
Does he get off not here
Grinning or anywhere.

❧ In the Booking Room

The man with the shopping bag is in so much trouble
He doesn't have nothing to do but have it he's had it
Before God knows and there's nothing to do about it
But set on a bench and wait for the rest of it
To come on down if it wants to and just keep on
Keeping on as usual holding the bag
With fourteen tubes of toothpaste and aftershave
And Brylcreem and Feen-a-mint now why would he want
He never boosted none of that they ask *him*
It was somebody left it there which he had nothing
To do with he must've picked it up like a bundle
You might find laying in the street and there's nothing else
Worthwhile doing but taking a good long look
At the floor and holding a handkerchief dripping blood
Tight over one ear like an empty seashell.

Breath Test

He isn't going to stand for it sitting down
As far as he can from the unshaded glare
And the TV camera where he isn't breathing
In no machine no thanks because no way
Being sober as a matter of fact his body
Without a warrant is nobody's damn business
And to a republic for which he isn't
Putting that thing in his mouth as a citizen
Who voted he has a right to disobey
The Law of Supply and Demand by running short
Of supplies and they can all go take a walk
On their own straight line all night if they feel like it.

To a Panhandler Who, for a Quarter, Said "God Bless You"

You held out your hand, expecting (on the average) nothing.
But when I crossed your palm with copper in an alloy sandwich
Newly minted by God's Country, you laid a misfortune
On me not even a prime-time gypsy would have thought of.

God bless *me?* *Me* be one for the cloud-capped, holy-
For-showbiz, smug, sharkskinny, hog-certain, flowery Chosen
Harping for glory? Thumbs-upping glissandos on pure-gold
    G-strings?
I couldn't stagger, let alone clodhop, to such music.

You could have said, *Heaven tempers the wind to the shorn lamb*
Or *Heaven will protect the working girl* or *Heaven*
Lies about us in our infancy. I half-swallowed those saws
Once. Their teeth stuck in my craw. Now I take wisdom
    sidewise.

Shorn lambs and working girls and infants over the years
Have taught me something else about Heaven: it exists
Maybe when the Corner-cutting Fleecer, the Punch
With the time clock, and the Unmilkable Mother aren't looking.

If God knows what's good for Him, He won't listen to you
About my anointment. He'll oil some squeakier sinner
And pour me an ordinary straight-up natural disaster.
Here's two bits more, palmer, to hope I'll be worth a damn.

❧ *Canticle for Xmas Eve*

O holy night as it was in the beginning
Under silent stars for the butchering of sheep
And shepherds, is now and ever shall be, night,

How still we see thee lying under the angels
In twisted wreckage, squealing, each empty eye-slit
Brimful of light as it was in the beginning

Of our slumber through the sirens wailing and keening
Over the stained ax and the shallow grave
That was, is now, and ever shall be, night

Of the night-light, chain and deadlatch by the bolt
Slammed home, the spell of thy deep and dreamless
Everlasting sleep as it was in the beginning

Of the bursting-forth of bright arterial blossoms
From the pastures of our hearts to the dark streets
Shining what is and shall be for this night

Of bludgeons and hopes, of skulls and fears laid open
To the mercies of our fathers burning in heaven,
O little town of bedlam in the beginning
Of the end as it was, as it is to all, good night.

❧ *Your Fortune: A Cold Reading*

*When a fortune-teller knows nothing in advance about a client,
he/she is forced to give a "cold reading," a fortune applying to
almost anyone, but sounding very personal.*

Say nothing revealing. You needn't tell
Anything about yourself or what you suppose
You are or were or what you're going to be.
Give away no secrets. While you sit there, trusting
Nothing you hear, you will hear your fortune.

This is your lucky day, but you don't know
Quite where to turn. Your life is approaching
A sudden climax, but making up your mind
Has always been hard for you. This lack
Of confidence has lost you chance after chance.

Too much of the strongest and most beautiful
Stays hidden in you, unused, neglected:
Your influential ease, your powers of persuasion,
And that gift of inborn charm (through no fault
Of your own) are largely unknown to those around you.

And you deserve far better than that. Now someone
Is coming toward you, older, gray-haired, dark-eyed,
To tell you wonderful news, but you won't listen.
Another person, shorter, pale-eyed, fair-haired,
Is lying to you, and until you know that fact

Your future is shadowed. You stay faithful in love
As long as your love is faithful, but you feel
Dissatisfied, unfulfilled. This nervousness
Is the pivot of your problems. Here at the turning
Point of your life, you must finally choose.

You are more sensitive and romantic now
Than you have ever been. You need love and attention,

But in spite of all you say or do, no matter
What you wear or how you groom your body,
Your heart, your mind, and what you trust is your soul

Feel strangely empty. You have someone only
Halfway into your life, half in strange dreams,
Who will not tell you whether you're close to parting
Or coming closer together. A would-be lover
Is waiting for you, but may soon give up hope.

You gave in once to the conventional world,
Taking its orders, obeying its rules, but lately
Because of your impulsive, heart-led nature,
You have begun to change and have suffered for it
From the tongues of neighbors and friendly hypocrites.

But soon you will learn to trust your own good judgment.
You will live long, be wealthier and wiser.
You don't know how unusual you are.
If you could have the answer to one question
Now, truly, secretly, what would it be?

✢ The Excursion of the Speech and Hearing Class

They had come to see the salmon lunging and leaping
Up the white spillway, but the water was empty.
Now one young girl lingers behind the others,
And slowly, her thin arms held out from her sides,
Alone on the riverbank, she begins to dance.

Her body moves as the salmon would have moved
In place, holding that place in a soundless calm
Under a soundless frenzy of surfaces
Against a current only she remembers
To welcome, to break through, to gather again.

The wind and the river pulse against her face
And under her feet. She listens to what they know
And moves her lips to find the mouth of the river
And the mouth of the slow wind against her mouth.
The source of the river and the source of the wind

Have taken her breath away. But the others come
Shaking their fingers, opening and closing
Their mouths, to take her back to another silence.

Sequence:
A Sea
Change

🌿

🌿 Going to Sea

Since we're setting out to sea, everything in our world
Has suddenly one of two clear, separate names:
What We Leave Behind
And What We Take With Us. We have no need to rehearse
    disasters,
Like being wrecked and stranded, to choose our cargo.
We were born marooned,
Have been castaways all our lives, practicing the survival
Of our fittest, and now we know what's necessary:
Relics of our bodies
And souls, what's left of our minds, remnants of our hearts,
And something more weatherproof than our bare skins
To hold between us
And the sun, the rain, and the wind which keep no promises
And no appointments, but which will surely arrive
With or without our approval—
Add food and water, and we can subsist on these alone
After a dying fashion. We make our X
At the crux of departure
And bury there all we no longer treasure: death's-heads

Over bones crossing like sabers, a dead man's chest,
Songs hollow as laughter,
Our pieces of eight and gold doubloons, our empty bottle
Left in the sand behind us, holding the message
Of our light parting breath.

❧ *At Sea*

We had always wanted to behave like the wind, moving
At its insistence slowly or quickly,
Obeying its impulse
Without regret under sails as full as clouds and taking
Gladly to heart its general direction.
The land disappears.
It sinks like an enormous ship. Even its mountains
Go back where they began, like us: under water.
Now our horizon
Levels the world, the mountains are made plain, and nothing
Is standing roughly upright except our mast
Which was once a tree
Among trees, its roots in a different element, growing
In the dark, opposed to changeable surfaces.
It answered gravely and lightly
The long calls of the earth and the zenith, and still aspires
But not to deeper or higher things: it leans,
It circles, quivers
As if ready to fall to the ax, shakily pointing
At the unreachable, unteachable sky,
Now there, now anywhere,
Trying to tell us too much but speaking only in whispers
Like its lost branches. If we knew where we were going,
It might be impossible
To get there with all this uncontrollable help from midair
And a tree whose needles have long since gone to ground

To find true north,
But having no destination makes our traveling easy
Going so far, so far. We should have forgotten
Long ago where to go.

❧ *Taking Our Bearings*

To find out where we are, we gaze at the sunset,
Then the moon and stars.
We bring their images down to touch the sea,
And there we are: there,
At a certain time where straight lines intersect
On a chart—that's you and I
In all this emptiness, the only two
In the world existing
Our way in this place. We can put our fingers
Surely on our uniqueness,
Call where-we-are what-we-are, letting it go
Finally that simply,
Saying again it's only the beginning
Again, it's only
The beginning of everything we always wanted
To do and know and be.
Bracing uncertain sea-legs, we breathe the salt
Of our own blood,
Pitching, heeling, and yawing with the unbreakable
Rules of this road,
And steer by constellations we needn't measure,
Name, or number.
One must keep watch now while the other sleeps,
Each dreaming of sharing
Dreams like our food or, through a dreamless night,
Sleeplessly waiting
For daybreak, sharing the naked love of dreaming.

It will mean we're becoming
Each other, replacing our dying mothers and fathers
And our own children,
Rocked in this wooden cradle of the deep,
By good dead reckoning
Leaving behind our streaming, luminous wake,
Sailing toward morning.

❧ The Calm

Drifting and mimicking the loss of the wind
With a loss of mind,
Left slack-sailed here in the sea, doing nothing at all
For days, we begin
Taking our lives uneasily. Only the daylight
And the cracked chronometer
Are moving. Though we turn away from the sun
Or rise under the moon
As if we were earth and tide, the rest is stillness.
If we broke our silence,
This palpable air would ripple obediently,
But our voices falter.
They melt on the sea, as brief as glints of starlight.
On the deep dry land.
Why did we never think of the miles and miles
Under us, holding us?
Above half-leagues of water, we think of little
Else than how deeply
The two of us might sink, turning to food
For the thoughts of others.
We could have stayed on firmament, on a desert
Where water waves goodbye,
Goodbye, and vanishes, a plain where it flows
On its own slight journeys,

Or on mountains where we could watch it frozen, toppling
(Instead of us) down cliffsides.
But here we huddle, surrounded. From miles below,
Now, come the monsters
Toward the glassy calm around us, uncoiling,
Lifting kelp-ragged
Slime-scaled snag-toothed cold impossible heads,
Eyes filled to the brim
With blankness, breaching and hulking, slewing toward us
Where we drift like lures.
Though they come closer, closer, blurred in the dark,
They never strike, never
Loom, ravenous, never thrash the surface
To break this mirror.

❧ *Reading the Sky*

Look, love, the sky is full again, as full as our sails.
Not being weather-wise, we read the baffling
Language of that sky
Slowly and doubtfully. Some skillful mariner might know
The signs like the palms of our hands and tell us
What we must do today
To be ready for tomorrow, but we murmur the names
Of clouds as if they were friendly enemies
Not meant to be trusted
To go where they should go or not to disguise themselves
Suddenly in different masks and colors.
The sky reminds us
Of our unpredictable minds: irresolute, inconstant,
Oracular, full of a mysterious music,
Barren, well- and ill-tempered.
Though we can't make it reveal its futures or our fortunes,
Here on the crests of waves that move us and move us

We can pay it honor:
We know its blues and reds, like our bodies, are born of dust,
Its whites and grays mere vaporings, its blackness
Concealed by dazzle,
But all this broken beauty of cloud-shapes, the endless
Promises and the unrepeatable gestures
Of light, omens, high masses,
Each shred, each smattering of each flamboyant sky-scape
Have numbed our language into a mawkish grandeur.
Though it may look absolute
For death to those beaten by storms, it can never be ugly
And never meager or miserly, always lavish
With unselfconscious praise
Of itself, even when empty. Let others people it
With hosts of maladroit gods, benign or vengeful,
Flinging stones or manna:
What it really is is gift and weapon enough. Though Heaven
Be lost or strayed or stolen, we have the heavens
Instead to venture beneath
From beginning to end, and though we come to the end of the
    earth,
The waterfall of the vanishing ocean, the dropping-off place,
We bear these heavens with us.

❧ *Landfall*

Our boat aground, we bring slow feet ashore, and they sink
But not in sand alone. They keep believing
In the sea: they rise
And fall, not understanding. They won't agree with the land
Or each other, stumbling sideways in memory
Of the waves now breaking
Calmly and raggedly behind us. We're upright, and we seem
To stand, and we turn like worlds half free of the world,

Small moons spinning near
Our mother, earthbound but dazed by distance. Have we come
    home?
Is this where we were born? Is this where it was
All along, this place
Where, again, we must learn to walk? We wallow from the water
Like our hesitant helpless curious ancestors,
Taking our first taste
Of the different air and kneeling awash as if to pray
For trust in what holds us up less yieldingly
After a sea change,
No longer buoyant, bearing the burden of inescapable
Heaviness among strangers who are already
Shyly coming toward us,
Asking what seem to be questions in an unknown language.
Is it what we've always asked ourselves? *Who are you?*
Can you be trusted?
What do you want? They hold their hands behind them, hiding
Flowers or knives. Love, remember not caring
Whether this was the end of us
When we set out, embarking on new lives with nothing
To lose but our names? Now all turns nameless again
For us who must love to learn
Once more how to point at the trees and birds and animals
We see around us, even our own hearts,
Naming, renaming them.

Five

✤ *The Song*

At first, he sang for love
Of singing and for one
Who laughed and wept and listened.

He sang to water falling
On sand and the steep woods
And streaming against stone.

He sang in the cold
For the lives and deaths of birds
And forests and elders.

And then he sang to be
Believed, waiting alone
Under a shut window.

On the shore, at the feet of trees,
By a creek, by a silent house,
He changed to what he sang

And became for a time nothing
But a voice in the distance
Touching the ears of others.

And now he sings again
For love in a way no stranger
Or lover will ever hear

Without remembering her
In his arms, no matter where
Or how that singing ends.

⚹ *In Love*

Before arriving at love, our only problems
Were what to do all day
And all night. Good works? Remembering our makers?
Perpetual prayer
At the grinding wheels of fortune or taking turns
Like the earth beneath us
From shadow to shadow? The passionate reenactment
Of pasts whose grievances
Seemed near and too dear, as sour as a miser's dream
Of gold from nowhere?
Or counting our sad blessings backwards to zero?
But now we sleep
And wake in the wildly abandoned countrysides
Of our bodies, embodying
Whole days and nights while Time keeps time, keeps time
With our preoccupied hearts.

Love Song After a Nightmare

Half listen, love, half asleep,
To the beginning of morning:
Your dream was the water,
And over its face, light air
Comes singing out of the shadows
Across a field to our house:
Birdsong and one shred
From the buried nest of the sun
Entering (dim and distant)
This room where you have spent
All you could spend on the night
And now lie empty-handed.

Your hobbled heart, heartbeaten
Through the terrible pasture,
Not led but driven
Straight to the still water
And under, now falters ashore
Out of your nightmare
Still breathing, still carrying
The burden of its proof:
You, with your fear behind you.

Though the sun may burn
Among crossed branches
At the grate of the window
Like our bodies around our bones,
Love has come back alive
To stretch its arms again:
It will need nothing more
Than what we bring together
On this, our next first day
On earth, to make its garden.

❧ *For a Woman Who Doubted the Power of Love*

Didn't I say the sun would cross the sky
Like a burning stone
And, like a burnt stone, fall in the evening
To light the pathway
Of the huge red stone of the moon rising
For our eyes only?
Didn't I say the moon would fade and leave us
Pale as our faces
Here at the end of night as we lie together
Under the drifting snow?
Didn't I say all snow would turn to water,
Each drop a flower,
That the sun would rise as molten as always
In time with birdsong
By the light of our moving arms in the morning?
My love, listen and learn
Once more how I did all this by the power
Of your heart and my heart.
How could the sky and these falling star-lit leaves
Catch fire without us?

❧ *Under the Sign of Moth*

Having read and written myself almost to sleep, I stretch
Toward the light and see it
There on the otherwise bare ceiling:
A rust-and-black-winged moth
Motionless over our heads, waiting for something—
The scent of a distant, screened-off mate? Some hint
Of a flower to feed on? Another chrysalis?

My wife is already sleeping, not knowing
We will spread our dreams under the Sign of Moth,
A constellation presiding over us
(More plausibly than the thread-spinning of stars
That housed our births) by clinging
Somehow to the plaster heaven we trusted
To see us safely and vacantly through the night.

I turn out the lamp that might have tempted it
To flutter down and play its familiar role
As a fool for brightness, a hopeful dabbler
Aspiring long enough to expire, battered
And singed by what it thought it wanted,
To suffer a last demeaning transformation
Into a moral lesson.

In the near-darkness, its eyes catch at the streetlight
And gleam deep red, lidlessly staring
Downward at the beginning of our sleep.
What can I offer it but peace and quiet?
With heavy eyelids, I return its gaze
More and more heavily, now blinking, my body
Unable to rise to this occasion,

Either to hunt for love or food or light
Or to fashion a moth-net from some gauzy remnant
Or to manage anything but a spinning fall
Into a dream of becoming

A shape that wants to leave old forms behind,
Now hidden, now crawling upward, now flying,
Endlessly new, endlessly unfolding.

The ceiling is blank in the morning.
I yawn and slip out from under, obeying the obscure
Scheme of the day, drifting from room to room.
The moth is somewhere in a dusty crevice,
Its long tongue coiled more certainly than a spring
Made to keep time, still waiting
For what it came to find and will die for.

𝒷 Ode to Twelve Yards of Unscreened Fill Dirt

The dump truck left the rough-and-tumble angles
Of your repose in the shape of my weekend:
A hundred cartloads of earth for me to move
From curbside to back yard to make a garden.

Among your clods like a curriculum vitae
In a kitchen midden: the corpse of an azalea,
A gunnysack, and pot shards from nursery days;
From wreckers' claims, rough nuggets of concrete;

From pastoral years, the blanched, beheaded root balls
Of buttercup and sorrel looking bewildered
By the shift of scene, by one more rearrangement
Of zenith and nadir at the turn of a spade;

And stones, from warblers' eggs to pterodactyls'—
All part of your bedload on another journey
Without the benefit of running water,
Mud flow, mantle creep, or freeze-thaw prying.

You've been here before as part of these foothills
Where the downpour of coastal storms and mountain snowmelt
Meet in crosscurrents. You aged on a forest floor,
Were washed from creek to river to floodplain,

Meandered to brushy swamp, and settled down
To pasture, holding your own. Now hold again
Young ferns and moss, the nurse-logs I bring to you,
Matrix of all beginnings. Come to bed.

❧ *Falling Asleep in a Garden*

All day the bees have come to the garden.
They hover, swivel in arcs and, whirling, light
On stamens heavy with pollen, probe and revel
Inside the yellow and red starbursts of dahlias
Or cling to lobelia's blue-white mouths
Or climb the speckled trumpets of foxgloves.

My restless eyes follow their restlessness
As they plunge bodily headfirst into treasure,
Gold-fevered among these horns of plenty.
They circle me, a flowerless patch
With nothing to offer them in the way of sweetness
Or light against the first omens of evening.

Some, even now, are dying at the end
Of their few weeks, some being born in the dark,
Some simply waiting for life, but some are dancing
Deep in their hives, telling the hungry
The sun will be that way, the garden this far:
This is the way to the garden. They hum at my ear.

And I wake up, startled, seeing the early
Stars beginning to bud in constellations.
The bees have gathered somewhere like petals closing
For the coming of the cold. The silhouette
Of a sphinx moth swerves to drink at a flowerhead.
The night-blooming moon opens its pale corolla.

❧ The Gardener's Dream

By moonlight he saw roses already climbing
Over the wall and into the wild fields
Where they budded and bloomed even as he was gazing
From the middle of the garden: foxgloves and columbine
Were lifting their stalks to blossom beyond his gateway
Downhill to a stream bed and across it into a forest
Among cryptantha, purslane, and bleeding heart.
Their seeds as they touched the earth were swelling and bursting
At once and rooting, unfolding, springing upward
Across a whole valley. The borders he'd planted and culled
As seedlings had sprawled out of order, their careful rows,
Their circles and squares and oblongs
Had gone astray and were stretching at random
Across his paths, their colors brightening
With stems and calyces brought back from the dead,
And almost at hand, pale flower heads turned to him
In the morning as if expecting light and rain
To spill from his fingers.

❧ *Caterpillar Song*

Summer and leaves filled me
With a green drowse, now full
Of sleep I must turn
Leaflike, the fine thread
Comes from my lower lip
And fastens to a leaf, I am
Weaving around my fullness
A closing, a slow shuttling
To touch there and there
Where I will dream
All my hearts withering
And changing to a half-remembered
One in the air who quivers
Among leaves, who will know
Night after night by this
Night I spin around us how
Already it stirs
From sleep inside me, gathers
The leaves I have left
In me, how we begin
Together, it grows huge eyes
For me, and we wait
Behind them, it is growing
Shut wings, we wait between them
Night by night after this
Night spun around us, we know
Now is the time to soften
The way ahead for us, it opens,
The wet shut wings come slowly
Out, they open, the veins
Fill them, they harden
And belong to us, we see
The night with all our eyes
At once, we move our wings

Apart among leaves, the one
Leaf with eyes to open
The night, not falling now
But rising and flying.

❧ Spider Song

It flies crookedly
For its food toward the heart
Of color. It will be bound
To touch my colorless
Round thin web-flower
Where I wait at the center
At ease even with wind.
And it comes now, caught
By the fine-spun petals
Where it waits, where it beats
Its wings. It waits
While I dance to help it
Wait, to learn to become
Something far different.
I hold it at the ends
Of what I am. It learns
To turn in one direction
Only, only to spin
One way under my eyes.
It learns to love
What is pale and quiet,
Near, motionless,
Whatever is here. It forgets
All those further places
That made it thrash and flutter.
It learns those wings
Were meant to bring it here.
It learns stillness. It turns
For a last time into me.

✹ *Moth Song*

I tasted it, the gold
In the gold, I saw the sweetness
At the end of my uncoiling
Tongue, by the beautiful ends
Of what curved from my forehead,
And I swam, gliding, I dove
Through the air toward gold
And sweetness meant to be
Chosen, begging to hold me
And be drawn inside me.

But I stop now, I hang
Still, suddenly suspended
Without having chosen to be
Still in a breeze still full
Of calling and beckoning
Red and blue around gold,
And what comes to meet me
Holds me and turns
My body, spinning a lightness
Around me to fold my wings
Close into a darkness,
And it turns me slowly
Into a flower and drinks me,
And I open, I become
Completely known, I blossom.

✵ *The Orchard of the Dreaming Pigs*

As rosy as sunsets over their cloudy hocks, the pigs come flying
Evening by evening to light in the fruit trees,
Their trotters firm on the bent boughs, their wings
All folding down for the dark as they eat and drowse,
Their snouts snuffling a comfortable music.

At dawn, as easily as the light, they lift
Their still blessed souse and chitlings through the warming air,
Not wedging their way like geese, but straggling
And curling in the sunrise, rising, then soaring downward
To the bloody sties, their breath turned sweet as apples.

ꙮ The Garden of Earthly Delights (after the painting by Hieronymus Bosch)

We stand in bright pools together, waiting with crows,
Some with white egrets, and some with leaf-winged apples.
Among us, our dark sisters. Some few are drowning,
But what does it matter? We are beautiful,
Our smooth temptations, our whiteness and blackness
Are being praised by the Pride of the Peacock,
And around us an endless penitent festival
Is riding its bears and camels, lions and goats,
Wild boars, gryphons, and unicorns, with roses deeper
Than our dreams, huge fish as emblems,
And the unbreakable egg of the Bird of Love.

Beyond them, the rarest birds, alertly at peace,
Larger than mere life, attend our pageant.
They see us born out of mussels and weedcrowns,
They see a few returning to sleep in shells,
They share the enormous berries we have learned
To crave as they do, to cling to, to carry
From one place to another, the dangling grapes
Which taught us to cluster, ripen, and drink
(Like moths from wild thistles) only to ourselves.

Why should we care what birds may want from us?
They have it at will, the seeds, the softening flesh
Of apples, strawberry beds, the arbors
Whose grapes burn dark as the moon on the other
Side of this earth that has made us the chosen
Attendants of its ceremonial daylight.
We live and die here hourly. We burn, we drift
From one invisible fire to the next, we fondle
What feeds our loving mouths with the first silence
We gave to what first gave us sweetness and sadness.

And we dance among them and find each other's bodies
Standing or lying down, all growing like fruit

And moving, swelling in this perpetual season
Of our fulfillment into comfortable Death
Whose towers we delight to climb, the pink and blue
Marble and flowering turrets risen from water
Like five Fortunate Islands where no laughter
Spills or gathers or takes leave of our senses.

Some idly take to the air as birds and go
Wherever they wish, some perch to wait our pleasure
Or take the paths all creatures, like constellations,
Take at their peril in this day with no evening,
This constant day in sheltered estuaries
We could visit easily if we wished to begin
Walking among the safely grazing and browsing
Beasts of the field and orchard and far forest.

Instead, we will stay here and become nothing
But what we are, the careless gardeners
Who scarcely touch the earth, who never smile.
Even the drowned, the confined, the suspended
Hold their unsmiling faces still forever.

❧ *Waking Up in a Garden*

We wake together, discovering the garden
Has gone to sleep around us, the sky dead black.
We've nearly forgotten
The when and where of love that brought us here
And left us near sundown, the why and how of our lives
At the familiar strange beginning of night.

The moths are hovering at the shadows of flowers,
Engrossed by their blurred labors, some zigzagging
Wildly, cross-purposefully,
And some in whorls like nebulae, constellations
Unstrung from the belt of their small zodiac
To fade and waver down into the grass.

And sweeping by, the bats are taking others
Silently and carefully into silence.
A nighthawk, the backswept
Outlines of its wings dark crescent moons,
Swoops near again and again. The moths vanish,
Reappear and vanish, die, spin back transformed,

And we lie under this feast like part of it,
Not wishing ourselves the sure wings of the hunters
But, lighter than feathers,
The baffling erratic uncontrollably crooked
Night-bearing gifted star-marked wings of the hunted
Whose tongues, like ours, go spiraling into sweetness.

❦ *A Woman Feeding Gulls*

They cry out at the sight of her and come flying
Over the tidal flats from miles away,
Sideslipping and wheeling
In sloping gray-and-white interwoven spirals
Whose center is her
And the daily bread she casts downwind on the water
While rising to spread her arms
Like wings for the calling of still more gulls around her,
Their cries intermingling at the end of daylight
With the sudden abundance
Of this bread returning after the hungry night
And the famine of morning
And the endlessly hungry opening and closing
Of wings and arms and shore and the turning sky.

❧ *A Woman Standing in the Surf*

Thigh-deep in the sea, she watches waves arriving
As if those storms
Thousands of miles away in starry spirals
Or the long upheavals
Of fire from the ocean bed or the almost breathless
Breathless baffling
Of winds by the moon had all been brought to bear
And to light on this shore
For her alone, each having known all along
Where she was waiting
And how to touch her coldly, billowing gently
Or suddenly surging
As she rises to meet them, crying out out of fear
Of her desire, in wonder
Outspreading her arms over water to welcome them
Against her, against her.

❧ *Lifesaving*

Those arms stretching toward you helplessly,
Beating the waves and clutching the air,
Want to hang on, they want to hold you close,
Closer forever, not out of love
But fear of losing a way of life by drowning.

No matter how reassuringly you say
To listen and trust you, to relax and give in
To the easy water lifting you together,
That mind staring at you and at nothing
Can't understand *why* it should stop screaming.

One hand is suddenly seizing you, half-strangling,
And one wild crook of an arm is locking
Around your head, and that mind is losing its mind.
Not losing yours, you do what the water
Around you has done already: you give way.

You go away from the light and air, you settle
Downward as if to end the world
Of the head and heart, taking the other with you
As far down as that body will follow
Into the darkness, and it lets you go.

It rises again to the uncertain surface,
No longer thrashing, no longer grappling
Or flailing, out of its wits, but desperately calm.
It believes you now. It's lying still
While your palm is lifting it gently, almost weightless,

The face aimed at the sky, the mind once more
Seeing and listening, remembering
To believe its body can float as well as yours,
That its arms and legs can begin to move
Surely with yours toward the land of the living.

❧ *That Moment*

Having swum farther than he'd known he could swim, so far
He'd stopped looking for land
And had simply gone on swimming and swimming till his arms
Slowed, exhausted,
And his legs, no longer fluttering, faltering out of time
With his heart, began
To settle slowly deeper and deeper into water
(For all he knew
Deeper than any water he'd ever crossed), that moment
His feet, instead of nothing, touch
The soft upflow of earth to bear them, and he starts breathing
Almost as if each breath
Might follow another, as if he could depend on knowing
From this breath forward
That his body, though nearly weightless, might move once more
Light-stepped, as buoyant
As light on the face of the moon, alive after all
That dying, that moment
He turns and walks toward her in a room, his love
For her that moment beginning.

❧ *A Guide to the Field*

Through this wild pasture, this mile of strewn grasses,
We walk among seed crowns
Only half-formed at the beginning of summer
But already growing
Heavier with the burdens nothing will harvest
But birds and the weather,
Some (this ryegrass) like caterpillars spinning
Cocoons out of sunlight,
And some (this lavender bluegrass) a waist-high forest
Of slender fir trees,
Still others (cheatgrass, wild barley) plotted like flowerbeds
Under flights and counter-flights
Of swallows and field sparrows. Each blade, each spikelet,
Each glume and awn, each slowly
Stiffening stem, no matter what may come
In the next wind—hail or fire—
Will take its beheading, will give up this year's ghost
With less than a murmur,
And we pass beside them now, taking together
Our first strange steps
On a path that leads us down to its end in water.
Each look, the first.
Each touch of our strange fingers, the first again.
Each movement of our bodies
As strangely startling as what the swallows dare
Skimming the pond, their wingtips
Glancing, glancing again, swept-luminous crescents,
Each act of theirs
As if for us only. They show us ways to turn
Into willing lovers
Not needing to say *Yes* on this day when all questions,
Even before the asking,
Have mingled with their answers. Remember winter:
Birds gone, seeming lost,
And the grass lying down once more to pretend one death,
Dried pale and brittle

By a hard-earned hard-learned gift of seeming done
With its life. Love dies, and love
Is born at the same heart-roots in words once cold
And comfortless as a scattering
Of ashes: *All flesh is grass* meaning *Love lies down*
Mortal, immortal.

✤ Getting Away

We had brought our love there: to a lake by a forest
And by nightfall at the firelit hearthstone lay
Together to whisper it, to become it,
To dream it. But something wanted out of the closet.

The rat-scratching began at the inner threshold,
Moved up the jamb and scratched at the lintel
And went scuffling left and right along bare walls,
Searching a way out but falling and scrabbling.

We had met life from the woods already, gray-and-white
Mouse-heads peeking tremulously between floorboards,
And had heard them tip-tailing carefully from spring
To spring in the loveseat, holding their nesting ground,

And in their behalf, and in love's, had decided to live
And let live, to share the bread we'd broken
Under this roof where they were as safe from claws
As we were from new preachments and old orders.

But this was no subtle mousy deferential
Skittering. It was an unabashed declaration
Of independence by something as good as lovers
At making and having its way and getting away.

We tried pounding the door, imagining wood rats
Like city rats would have the self-regard
To quit and go into hiding and come back later
When they would have themselves to themselves like us.

But the scratches went on, not pausing, went on
And on without fear, without flinching, without shifting
To the ceiling or underfoot on whatever passage
This fellow creature had gnawed and wriggled through.

So at last with brooms and boots and the righteous courage
Of tenancy (our self-possession being
Nine points of our law) we braced ourselves
To face the tenth, having propped the porch door wide

To tempt it into the hospitality
Of the night where it would be welcome naturally
And opened the closet door, while cringing sideways,
And saw the tawny-backed slender snow-breasted weasel

Standing erect, the small paws dangling, gazing
From brooms to us more calmly than possible
And tilting a small incredibly sinuous head
And neck on its shoulderless body, slowly deciding

To let us go on being where we were
Whatever we were, whatever we meant to be,
And it bent at the baseboard and glided on all fours
Around the corner and out the door down the stairs

More smoothly and silently than the evening
Had climbed them, and disappeared into the darkness
And left us and the mice in that good house
Where nothing stirred but all of us till morning.

❧ *Our Blindness*

I see you now, and now
With the sudden end of lamplight
At the bedside have lost you
For a brief while to the night
Except for the pale drift
Of the pillow beside your face
And, over your landscape,
The softly touching whiteness
Of the sheet like a bed of snow.

Now love is blind. We move
To find what we can't see
Across the strange familiar
Neighborhood of our bodies
Like the blind when a snowfall
Has muffled and smoothed away
All shapes from their feet and fingers
To make a second blindness.
We turn to all we know.

℀ *By Starlight*

Now far from those harsh lights and the glare over cities, alone
By a clearing in a forest, we lie down
For the first time in our lives
Together under stars
And, keeping the earth in its place behind our backs, we stare
Upward into the ancient stream of starlight
Whose current, though it appears
To falter, to waver,
Has made its way to our eyes through barely imaginable
Down-curved ravines of space to dazzle us
With its streamers and wildfires,
Its ice-laden glitter,
The unconstellated burning rubble of godlings, outcast
And spilled from the zodiac and constantly falling
As they have always fallen
Even before eyes turned
To wonder and will go on falling whether we stay to watch
Or soon give back our small share of the spectrum
To the oldest of nights, to the expansive
Gestures of a universe
We share so pointedly: some (see there) bloomed long ago
And dimmed, yet shine through lifetimes without a source,
With no beginning left
Behind them now
To begin with, but only an ever-shortening reach of glory
That flickers in darkness. All will consume themselves
And be reborn, as we are
Here, having followed
Their example, love, as fixed and erring and fair and steadfast,
Not star-crossed yet, but truly catching them
As they slant to us past hemlocks, as rich
And clear as our silence.

✿ *For a Third Anniversary*

You brought me wildflowers once, not the real ones
You'd learned and loved after school along the roadside
April by April, after the city fathers
Had cut them down—*poppies and vetch, pentstemon*
And bleeding heart—not the ones you'd gathered
For other grudging teachers who'd held your life
And your life-to-be too lightly, but words in a poem.

You set them down so gently, so carefully,
So quietly, I almost didn't notice
They were saying goodbye to me. *Cut flowers,* you said,
Rootless. Bright awkward moments already wilting.
No sweets, no charms, no dancing, you said, but words
Like flowers, *removed from life.* A lesson in loss.

Years late, into the yard behind the house
We share, I bring my answer: river stones,
Deer fern, moss, and stumps from forest floors,
Survivors of neglect and mayhem, like words.
From among them, from what seemed a barren garden
As bleak as hope, come yellow violets,
Starflowers, and wild red currant.

❧ *In a Garden at the End of Winter*

On the pond, star-points of rain.
The hour before dawn, under fir
And cedar. River stones
Laid out like creekbeds
Downstream to nowhere, the heaviest
Half-buried, now halfmoons.

Spirals of young fronds waiting
At the hearts of sword ferns. Moss bedded
Still in its own night
But spread like green shade. Not one
Flower but shoots of wild roses
Budding dark red.

Towhee and song sparrow hidden
In a nest of nests, low among roots
Of a fallen pine. Ground squirrel
Deep under its nurse log, amber eyes
Half shut. The first half-broken
Croak of a tree frog.

Loud from the woods nearby, *Who? Who?*
Who ARE *you?* and louder still
From a branch straight overhead
Who? Who? Who ARE *you?*—one spotted owl
Already gliding wide-winged toward the other,
Knowing the answer.

❧ Turning Back and Starting Over

I
Our feet slow down by themselves, trudging reluctantly,
And we're stopping cold, even before deciding
To stop. And here we are:
For all these miles, we've been going the wrong way. That easy
Beautiful open downsloped welcoming trail
Was a hanging valley,
And now we stand at the sheer, sheared-off edge of it, staring
Down on the green place where we wanted to be
But have no path to.
Like unfledged hawks on a nesting ledge, we test our eyes,
Keen for the promises of worlds beyond us.
There they lie
Out of our reach, the grasslands strewn with lakes, the sheltering
Orchards like windbreaks where we might have rested
For the rest of our days
Instead of traveling, no matter how lightly. So we turn
Around regretfully and begin retracing
Our steps, those carefree
Rambling paces we took for granted, each now a dead loss,
A taking-back of what we once believed in
Wholly, wholeheartedly.
We search for the faint record of slips of heel and toe
On this hard stretch, on these unimpressed stones,
Seeing little or nothing
Of what we thought was progress: a few bent weeds, grass
    leaning
The wrong way here and there in our memory
Though not in our honor,
Scuff marks and all our slipshod blunders longer-lasting
Than any surefooted strides. What did we bring
To light or life? We put down
Only our feet, dislodged a few fragments, left some seedlings
Tilted out of their zenith-seeking longing
Temporarily.
Though we gave ourselves a name when we began—Explorers—

Now, starting over, we have two more to carry:
Backtrackers, Beginners.

2

We've returned to the place where we went wrong, seeing no
  sign
To mark the spot, no X to commemorate
Our long mistake,
And taking the first new step is as hard as the first step
We took as children, our hands held up in the air,
Believers praising
Our imminent rescue from all fours. Starting once more,
We have to forget how wrong we were back there
Or we might never
Move at all, but simply stoop or crumple, settling
For less and less in a heap, giving up, giving in
To the luxuries of failure,
Of never having to choose or try. Instead, we labor
Uphill, both forcing and reenforcing our share
Of haphazard fortune, wonders
Of a kind, here among greater wonders: all these boulders,
These astonishing stumbling blocks where we don't happen
To stumble this time, believing
In beginner's luck all over again. We've forgotten
On purpose, successfully, how to fail
And don't remember
Anything but the pleasures of traveling on and on
Though they may lead us now into nothing more
Amazing than dead-endings.

⚘ *Replanting a Garden*

Here, roses sickened in the shade of a house
Where only north light or the last light of evening
Could reach them. They would grope for a season,
Then molder and thin out, as flowerless
As moss and quillwort covering their roots
Or fungus caring for their slow deaths like nurslings.

So day by dawn, by storm or half-clouded sky,
He made his way through the woods
Where the dense crowns of fir and hemlock closed
A shade still deeper than house-shade, where sun
And rain fell, not as themselves, but as each other
(Light showers of light, light rain) to the forest floor.

And he knelt there to sword fern and deer fern,
Oak fern and holly fern, unearthing them gently
And wrapping their cool rootstocks for transplanting.
From the lips of pools, from creek banks and spring banks
And the feet of watersheds (their supple black-stemmed
Aureoles wavering) he brought maidenhair

And took whole sides of crumbling stumps in his arms,
Each bearing clusters of wood fern and shield fern,
And brought them home and laid them down in the garden
And stood beside their deepening, changing forms,
One earthbound frond at a time all summer long
Uncoiling life after life out of that shadow.

❧ *Downstream*

We give in to the persuasions of the river, floating
Swiftly downstream as well as the leaves beside us,
Ahead of us, with little choice
Which way it may be next
That we find ourselves
One boat-length farther along, taking the rough with the smooth,
To the slackness of pools, down long, eddying riffles,
To the rush of spillways narrowing
And steepening suddenly
To white water
Where the river is leaving everything to chance and turning
Over and interrupting its own half-motions
Constantly in bursts and arches,
Mantling, spun into tendrils,
Its wild gestures
As memorable at a glance as marble but dying, reborn
Only another glance away, as the center
Of our attention, shifting at random
Everywhere like the sunlight,
Is caught by the play
Of light on all these surfaces, churnings and interweavings,
Upheavals, blossomings, an impulsive garden
Where we search and search as if for answers
And see its one reply:
Nothing is the same
Ever. This intricate bewilderment of currents,
In its least ripple, is unrepeatable.
The windbreak of alders we pass now,
The gravely leaning pale-boned
Row gone ashen,
Love, is another river, its bed channeled by seasons.
Our faces come near each other, mysterious
As water always. We cross a pool,
Translucent, the stones below us
Glimmering, remaining.

❧ The Resting Place

We'll find it at the edge of a forest
Where moss and ferns, no longer overshadowed
By trees, will yield to grass, where a small stream
Will make its way among hills, where hills sliding
Like cross-waves into valleys (more pale
As they give in to distance) will turn to mist
Under the jutting folds of mountains
Whitened against the sky or steepened to blue
As far as blue-white clouds. And we'll rest there.

At our feet, the water will move in a grave dance,
Dissolving its stones downstream and honoring
Each one in its way for paying an easy tribute.
Nearby, a thrust of rock will remind us
Of the hard start of the earth. The weeds and wildflowers,
The bushes and brambles rooted for lost seasons
Will lose their names in the flourishes of the wind,
And our two natures, lost in thought,
Will give themselves away and become nameless.

We'll find an end to sitting and thinking,
Even to holding still, though stillness will be
That end in itself. Our reclining bodies,
Our longing and belonging shapes, will need
Nothing, will have nothing to wait for,
But will share the sun with other surfaces
Out of their depth, our eyes and fingers
Catching the sky as it falls and scatters
Around us, against us, its extravagant light.

❦ *First Light*

Before first light no sound
From the woods or the calm lake
Steel-gray in mist to its end
And even the creek's down-rush
On a stone bed gone still
As the owl that spoke for us
All night out of the hemlocks.

But now from the forest floor
(Dark green in a slow rain)
The voice of the winter wren—
Just as a touch of sun
Enlightens this good morning—
Begins its long cascading
Spillways and white rapids.

I see you wake, not moving
More than your eyelids
To listen, still half-held
By your dream, which was also mine
Between the owl and the wren:
That we'd learned how to fly
And sing by dark, by daylight.

You see my eyes have opened
With yours. Each of us turns
To the other, arms outstretched,
Then closed, both newly fledged
But as wing-sure at wakening
As owl-flight or wren-flight
And as song-struck as this dawn.